Journey with Jillian

Safe Passage through the Land of Suffering

Joyce Heil

Journey with Jillian: Safe Passage Through the Land of Suffering

Cover Design by Sarah Froggatt

Printed and bound in the United States of America

First edition

ISBN 978-0-692-44350-7

FOR JILLIAN

AND

FOR ALL

WHO FIND THEMSELVES TRAVELING

A SIMILAR ROAD

Special thanks
to my family for allowing me
to tell our story,
to those who walked
with me and with Jillian
on this journey,
and to my gracious editors:
Kathryn Royster
and Brian Beise.

CONTENTS

Art and Cover Design

by Sarah Froggatt

(Jillian's cousin)

Introduction

"Shall we accept good from God, and not trouble?"
Job 2:10 (New International Version)

Jillian would be in her twenties by now: a young woman with auburn hair, long legs, and a spray of freckles across her nose. Instead, she died in 2005 at the age of eleven. On an unseasonably warm day in a Nashville winter, we gathered with friends around a plain pine box to say goodbye to our daughter's broken body. It was the end of a long journey, a journey we knew would end this way, a journey we did not choose.

Although Jillian started out as a healthy and easygoing baby, at six months of age, she began to slow in her development, eventually losing any milestones she had gained. Her peaceful and engaging personality turned angry, confused, and detached. We desperately sought medical intervention and therapy, only to discover that she had Rett syndrome, a regressive illness caused by a random genetic mutation. The diagnosis crashed over us like a wave, while Jillian continued to sink in her collapsing world. With Rett syndrome, which primarily affects girls, the child appears normal at birth, but eventually slows in development. Then, sometime between six and eighteen months, she begins to regress. The regressive phase can last days or even months. Jillian's lasted more than a year. At the end of it, she was left at the developmental level of a one-month-old baby, able only to turn her head. She could not roll over, sit, crawl, talk, or feed herself. Once we had the diagnosis, we devoured all the Rett information we could find, trying to see what the future held for Jillian. We learned that, following regression, Rett girls typically regain at least some milestones; often, they even return to their previous level of development. Some Rett girls can walk or feed themselves. Because of the severity of her case, however, Jillian never regained any physical skills. We took her to more therapy and adjusted to being a family of a child with special needs. Jillian, so peaceful and beautiful with her reddish curls, made friends easily without playing or talking.

Most Rett girls have a span of peaceful years from preschool age though young adulthood, although some die early of complications. Sadly, Jillian's body continued to deteriorate to the point that I could not see a way for her to enjoy life through her discomfort. One January weekend, eleven-year-old Jillian lay in bed, sick with a viral illness. She started having difficulty breathing and we took her to the hospital, where her heart developed an irregular heart rhythm. Within an hour, she had died. Abruptly, our beautiful daughter was gone and our joyful, painful journey was over. The aftershocks of her death would continue for months and even years, but our time with Jillian was over.

To an outsider, Jillian's life as a child with profound special needs could seem tragic and our parenting of her a heavy burden. However, Jillian did not suffer in vain, as she had a full life that impacted many. Being her mother, I entered the land of suffering with her, and I was not alone. I thought I knew the triune God well—feeling safe in the Father's love, modeling my life after Jesus, listening to the promptings of the Holy Spirit. But in the land of suffering, I plumbed a new depth of spiritual understanding about life, worth, and the heart of God.

Shortly after Jillian was diagnosed with Rett syndrome, I had a conversation that set the tone for the road ahead. Through a support network, I called another mom who had a daughter with Rett syndrome. Her child, now a teenager, was named Abigail. After we had talked about our girls and I had asked many questions, this mother told me, "Abigail is the greatest blessing in my life—and I would change it in a minute if I could." Through her words, I caught a glimpse of the tension she lived with daily: to receive and enjoy all the blessings of her daughter while still acknowledging the reality of her suffering.

Life with a child who has severe special needs is like living in the Arctic or the desert. Both are barren landscapes. Every animal in these domains lives on the edge of survival, with food scarce and weather a constant threat. People who live in these places, if they adapt their lifestyles, discover the hidden gifts of the wilderness: quiet, simplicity, focus. But many people, especially those who come unprepared, perish in these places. Few people stay unless they have to, and fewer still *want* to live there. But those who stay experience incredible beauty. Similarly, my family's journey through the land of suffering brought treasure that could be discovered no other way.

I wrote this book at the encouragement of a pastor. He believes in healing and prays for it with faith. He has seen healings and miraculous events over his lifetime. After a service where I heard him invite people to get prayer for healing—which I supported—I wanted him to encourage those in the congregation who did not get healed that God is still working miracles. I shared with him the transforming work that Jesus did in and through Jillian, as well as others "not healed" or rescued throughout history. He said I should write it down. My prayer for anyone reading this is that you will be encouraged to trust God in your suffering, yield to it, and see what is birthed through it, even as you cry out for deliverance.

Chapter 1

The Journey Begins

Birth Through Diagnosis

Where can I go from your Spirit?
Where can I flee from your presence?
If I go up to the heavens, you are there;
If I make my bed in the depths, you are there.
If I rise on the wings of the dawn,
If I settle on the far side of the sea,
Even there your hand will guide me,
Your right hand will hold me fast.

If I say, "Surely the darkness will hide me
And the light become night around me,"
Even the darkness will not be dark to you;
The night will shine like the day,
For darkness is as light to you.

Psalm 139 (NIV)

Jillian joined our family in 1993, the third of four children. My husband Paul was (and still is) a pediatrician in Nashville, and our boys Luke (age 4) and Andrew (age 2) were delighted with the thought of a baby to love. I first saw Jillian on an ultrasound screen in South America. Early in my husband's career, we committed to going to Ecuador for one month every year so Paul could assist at a hospital in Shell, a village on the edge of the jungle. This hospital had about thirty beds and served the local area as well as patients flown in from the jungle. Some of the missionary staff, including our family, lived in an area separated from the hospital by a long swinging bridge that spanned a rainforest gorge. On our second trip to Shell, in July 1993, I was pregnant with Jillian, and our boys were three and two years old. Not long into our stay, we were given a gift, which I chronicled in a letter to Jillian for her baby book:

> In Ecuador, God gave us an unexpected treat. I love ultrasounds—just to see what God is forming in my belly. For financial reasons, we had decided not to have one with you unless we needed it. So I had completely died to the idea. Well, Shell had just received a new ultrasound machine, and a few days after we arrived, a visiting radiologist from Illinois came to show the doctors here how to use it. And they needed volunteers to practice. So here we were in a hospital room on the edge of the jungle with three doctors and an Ecuadorian resident watching you for the first time! Everyone was excited because they were learning, and they took their time because they wanted to find everything and measure it. I cannot explain what a joy it was for us both to watch

> you—your heart, your back, your legs. You are wonderfully made! Our OB report is in Spanish, and we have some snapshots of you with Hospital Vozandes del Orient on them. I smiled big the whole walk home over the swinging bridge.

Just four months after our return home from Ecuador, Jillian arrived. Her peaceful birth seemed to foreshadow an easy transition for our family, and indeed, she rarely cried and brought great joy to everyone. I remember hosting a lunch for friends a few months after Jillian's birth, and she lay on her back in the crib next to the group of talking women, so content, quiet, and observant. I continued writing letters to her for her baby book, trying to capture specific moments and glimpses I knew I would forget with time. In February, when she was three months old, I wrote about a church retreat I attended:

> At the retreat, we were supposed to bring a "treasure" to share with the other ladies—something special God had done for us. I brought a picture of you. I didn't get to share because time ran out, but in the process of deciding what I would say, I was overwhelmed with my love for you and God's goodness to me in sending you. I have so enjoyed you. You seem to want to communicate so much. When you were a few weeks old, you got conjunctivitis and needed eye ointment. It made your eyes soupy and messy. A baby that young doesn't give back much personal feedback, she just reacts to needs like hunger and sleep. You were sitting in your bouncy chair one day with your eyes gooped up and I walked over to you and spoke. You turned your head and craned

> and peered to look at me! I was so moved—my heart filled up with love and joy. Since that time you have continued to grow and desire connection with me and others. All babies coo and laugh, but you seem to converse and you thrive on it. You speak, wait, respond, grin, laugh, listen, leg-kick, tongue-out, wait, coo, wait, coo, wait, coo, smile! And how it tickles our hearts! The boys squeal in delight, "Jillian smiled at me!"

Also in Jillian's baby journal, I wrote poems about the boys and their relationship with their six-month-old sister. They show how quickly and easily she became an integral part of our family. As a four-year-old, Luke loved to help me take care of Jillian.

Who likes to hold your hand and cover little cold feet?
Who likes to snuggle close but cries when you pull his hair?
Who gives you kisses before he leaves for school,
And yells for mom when you spit up your food?
Who danced when you got a tooth
  and sits by your bouncy chair?
Who brings you toys and makes a silly face,
  just to see you smile?
Who doesn't like to hear you cry and hates it when you yell?
Brother Luke declared, long before your birth,
"There aren't many girls here—let's have a girl!"
And since you came into this world, a day does not go by,
That Luke does not pour his love out and hold you tight.

Andrew, nearly three, already devoted much time and energy to this new relationship.

"I love my Jillian!" Andrew says to me most every day.

And how your face lights up when you see his rosy cheeks.
People say you look alike and I think they are right.
He gently wipes your downy head and steals a little kiss
And beams with joy when anyone asks, "Who's this?"
"She's my Jilly Billy!" he answers with delight.
I love to hear him announce with glee, "Jillian's awake!"
And quick he rushes in to greet you and peek through
bumper pads,
While you kick, talk, and smile.

By the time Jillian was eight months old, she was charming everybody she met. In July 1994, I wrote:

> Everyone says, "What a good baby she is!" and I nod yes. You are so flexible, interested and amiable. We spent a week in Iowa, and you delighted everyone with your rocking on your hands and knees. So desperate to move! But you've learned to flop down and try again. Eventually you get where you want to be. Tonight I watched you rock and "whoomph" until you got to your mirror. After much smiling and conversation, you knocked it over and moved on to something new.

Over the next two months, however, Jillian's developmental milestones arrived more slowly. Earlier, at six months of age, we had noticed her slightly poor muscle tone. According to her doctors, however, she was still within normal range, so I dismissed the first tremors of worry, thinking she would improve with time. Between six and nine months, babies usually learn grasping, pointing, babbling, rolling, sitting, and standing. Jillian could hold broccoli in her fist and get it to her mouth, but she had difficulty picking up cereal with her fingers. She could only sometimes roll over. She could sit when supported but would then fall over. She would say “Da-Da” one day, and it would be gone the next. I told myself, “She's just not motivated to push herself—the boys are always entertaining her.” When Jillian turned nine months old, we traveled to Ecuador again. Several of the missionaries had children around her age, and I noticed that she did not play like her peers. Maybe because I was out of my normal routine, her developmental delay seemed obvious, and we resolved to seek help when we got back to Nashville. I wrote this on our return:

> Since we’ve been back, you’ve moved on to a new set of toys and you can scoot where you want to go. You can sit pretty well; you don’t like baby food much, and you’re relearning to sleep all night. Soon Grandma Harrison will be here to share a room with you so you must not wake at night! I can’t think of many “awesome” things you’ve done, but your presence is so refreshing. You endear yourself to others. I love doing things with you. Your brothers still delight in you. You are full of grace.

I believe that God prepares us in advance for what He allows to come our way. Sometimes we realize at the time what He is doing, but more often it is in retrospect that we can see His kind hand making a way for us. Paul and I suspected that Jillian, now ten months old, had some small developmental problem, so we made an appointment to see a neurologist.

The week prior to the appointment, during an extended visit from my mother-in-law, a friend from college stopped by. I had not seen this friend for several years and was eager to spend time with her and her new baby. As she walked up the front steps into my home, I looked at her baby in his carrier. He was so strong and bright, straining to get out of his car seat. He was younger than Jillian, and in that instant I knew that something was very wrong with my daughter. I could hardly entertain my friend. Thoughts were crashing around in my head, and grief was taking over my heart. It was like a veil had been pulled away, and I could see how broken Jillian was. I do not use denial as a coping mechanism, so I believe God protected me from the weight of this reality until it was time to carry it. When my friend left, I turned to my mother-in-law and began to sob. She had also noticed the difference between Jillian and my friend's baby. Without many words, she simply stood in that place of grief with me.

Over the next few days, Paul and I confronted the possibility of Jillian having special needs. We prayed and cried and huddled with friends. By the time we arrived at the neurology appointment, we were ready to hear what the doctor had to say. I don't remember the appointment taking very long. There were the usual questions about her activity: does she sit, can she crawl, does she clap, bring objects to midline, etc. Then he tested her reflexes, like all pediatricians do with their little hammers. In spite of her overall low muscle tone, her leg jumped more than it should have. Her arms showed the same hyper-reflexes, a sign of spasticity and brain injury. This doctor had literally written the book on pediatric neurology and had been one of my husband's instructors in medical school. He looked at us with sympathy and confirmed what we knew in our hearts. He was unwilling to speculate beyond the simple diagnosis of brain injury. Time, he said, would tell us more. Because we were not shocked, we were able to ask questions. I asked if this was cerebral palsy, and he said we could call it that for now. My feelings that day were of great heaviness and even physical nausea, but I also had unshakable peace. There was no panic, just the deepest grief I had ever touched. We went to church that night and cried as our pastor prayed for Jillian and for us.

Our pastor wasn't the only one to minister to us that night. I had recently begun attending a Bible study for young moms, and Dabney Mann, the group's leader, saw me sitting alone in the worship center and sat down next to me. She asked me what was going on, and I poured out the story of my day. She cried with me, hugged me, held my hand, said she was so sorry, and simply sat with me until class was over. I was grateful that God had provided this "mother" in His house to come and mother me during my dark hour. Neither my husband nor I had any family in town, and already God was raising up people to help us! Dabney and her husband Doug walked with Paul and me through the remainder of Jillian's life, cheering us on, loving us and our kids, and giving us counsel for the journey.

At home that night, I added an entry to Jillian's baby journal:

> Today was a hard day for us. Dad was especially hard hit, since he's really suspected something since you were 3 or 4 months old. In a week, we go to have an MRI of your brain to see if anything specific can be found. So these are the cold, gray facts, but God continues to be faithful.

Because different babies display a wide range of "normal" development in the first year, Paul had suppressed his occasional misgivings. Now he knew he had seen the early signs.

A few days later, I wrote:

> After several days of "mourning" normal development, telling family and friends, crying and receiving comfort, we have been greatly encouraged. On Sunday, following several days of illness, you woke up from your nap so alive! You tried to reach things above you; you smiled and laughed; you "crawled" around the kitchen, grabbed my leg, and explored the pantry. You held an "Aaah" conversation with Andrew back and forth, and wanted to be picked up. Since then you've been extra busy exploring, playing with your brothers, wanting to be with us, and so dear! How good God is. He has greatly encouraged us and given us delightful times with you. We so much want to stand in the gap for you, pray for your development physically, emotionally, spiritually, and not let Satan have any victory; but we are also so pleased with who you are, and we enjoy you everyday.

We go to a church that believes God still performs miracles today, and we had seen Him act powerfully in our lives. So now I turned to Him and prayed for Jillian. As I questioned Him as to whether He would heal her, or whether she would get worse, I felt Him with me. I did not feel alone or abandoned, ignored or unheard. But He also did not respond directly, as if He were silently looking at me with sad eyes that communicated what I did not want to hear. Throughout our journey with Jillian, as we sought His face for healing, I frequently felt this same presence: a tender, grieving compassion that nevertheless answered "no." But Paul and I did not give up hope, and we continued to pray for her complete or even partial healing because we knew He could do it. As King David said after praying for his dying son, "I thought, 'Who knows? The LORD may be gracious to me and let the child live'" (2 Samuel 12:22, NIV). I began to see that great suffering and spiritual challenges lay ahead. More than the doctors' diagnoses and therapists' exercises, this inner sense that Jillian would not be healed began to shape my outlook for her and our family. I wrote a letter in the new year, knowing Jillian was impaired but not yet aware that she had Rett syndrome. It begins with:

> My dearest Jillian,
>
> Writing in this book for you is going to be a little different than it was for the boys. I will still write about the joys of things you do or about places we go together. I will still select some of my favorite pictures and mount them. I will still include pertinent scripture and illustrations generated out of my relationship with God. But this journey you and I are on is bittersweet. And so your book will be different, as it will contain the unfolding of this journey.
>
> I am deeply rooted in God's immeasurable love for us both. And I am so thankful for who you are. You daily bless me, your contentment instructs me, your peaceful joy ministers to me. And yet as we go to doctors and therapists and I watch you try to wave or reach a toy, I go up and down. At one moment I am hopeful and encouraged, the next I am grieving and full of fear.

Our busy lives did not allow Jillian's condition to take all our time. I had two young boys who needed to be picked up at preschool and taken to the park and fed and enjoyed. Jillian herself was usually happy to be swept along with them to church, the grocery store, or play dates. At times things seemed normal. Then I would be confronted with Jillian's problems at night when she screamed, or when I did therapy exercises with her at home. I felt like my life was a house with different rooms full of good things, people, and experiences, and most of our life occurred in these rooms. But one room with a shut door, the room of Jillian's disability, was a place of grief and heartache. I had to go into that room, not alone but with Jesus, to deal with medical information and conflicting theories, my hopes and dreams, and my fears and expectations. This compartmentalization helped me keep my emotions in check and refocused me on the person of Jillian and her ultimate formation as a child of God, independent of her disabilities. I concluded the letter:

> I need to pray for your future with God. Physical and mental development, and emotional too, are secondary to spiritual. What destiny does God have for you? What of His nature has He planted in you? Why are you with us? Why did He allow you to be hurt? What does He want to show us through this? O Lord show us, teach us, protect our little girl.
>
> "His pleasure is not in the strength of the horse
> nor his delight in the legs of a man;
> the Lord delights in those who fear him
> who put their hope in His unfailing love."
>
> Psalm 147:10-11 (NIV)
>
> Today we picked you up at church, and you were in a jolly mood. You laughed easily, enjoyed your lunch (as

> we practiced chewing, biting, drinking, and spoon feeding), played with Mama's face, bounced on your haunches, talked up a storm and tried to be where the boys were. You looked beautiful in your dress, and you felt like a girl as I carried you in from the van. Your features are delicate and well formed. How I treasure the sum of them!

At this time, Jillian had not regressed, so we thought she had a static brain injury and would continue to make slow progress. Cerebral palsy is a so-called static brain injury diagnosis: it indicates that the child's brain was injured sometime prior to or during birth, either through infection, lack of oxygen, or trauma. A child with cerebral palsy spends the rest of his or her life recovering from that initial injury and its complications, but the injury itself is a past event. The child's condition usually remains stable or improves rather than worsening. Paul and I thought this diagnosis didn't quite match Jillian's medical history, but it did offer motivation to begin therapy. Immediately, my weeks became full of physical, occupational, and speech therapy appointments, all attended with my two small boys in tow. Physical therapists worked on crawling and sitting, and they made molded plastic orthotics to keep her heels from tightening up. Using toys adapted with big, easy-to-press buttons, speech therapists tried to determine whether she understood cause and effect. They also worked on swallowing and eating foods with different textures. Occupational therapists focused on her grabbing and grasping abilities and on sensory integration through feeling various materials. And she did make progress. By her first birthday, Jillian could sit awkwardly with her leg propped under her. She could crawl across a carpet and knock down a stack of blocks. She could laugh and clap and look us in the eyes and smile. She smiled most when her daddy applauded her efforts. At her birthday party, she opened her presents and ate cake. I was cautiously hopeful, poring over the boys' baby calendars and comparing Jillian's accomplishments to theirs.

To accommodate government requirements, every new therapist performed an "intake evaluation" to determine Jillian's baseline. They asked about developmental markers such as pointing, self-feeding, and making sounds. One of these intake questions was "Does your child clap?" As I tried to answer it one day with yet another new therapist, my thoughts started to race: *Yes, she claps . . . Wait . . . When was the last time she clapped? Was it this week? Did she clap last week? How long has it been? Can she still clap?* Suddenly, I realized that she had not done several things recently that I knew she could do. Was she losing ground? The answer came right after she turned one. She could crawl on her birthday. Shortly thereafter, she got a cold with a fever and was as lethargic as any sick one-year-old would be. As she got better and her energy returned, I waited for her to crawl again. She never did.

Now the doctors began to consider the possibility of a progressive brain injury, where the brain receives an initial injury and continues to deteriorate as the child grows. Progressive brain injuries are caused by genetic problems and include metabolic illnesses and regressive syndromes, where the child loses developmental milestones he or she had previously gained. These months after her first birthday were marked by poor sleep – Jillian screamed for hours every night. My days became a blur of sleep-deprived wishful thinking that she was fine, alternating with panicked apprehension that things were falling apart.

When Jillian was about 14 months old, Paul called a physician friend who worked in the Child Developmental Program at Vanderbilt University. They discussed Jillian's medical history on the phone, and Paul mentioned almost as an aside that her feet got very blue in the bathtub. Paul's colleague suggested a possible diagnosis of Rett syndrome. Paul, having only been in practice a few years, had never seen a child with Rett syndrome. He vaguely remembered it as a "bad" diagnosis and thought surely Jillian's developmental delay was not that severe. But he set up an appointment for Jillian to be seen by his colleague. The week before the appointment, he brought home information about Rett syndrome, including case studies. It sounded like Jillian: normal birth and infancy, followed by delayed development turning to regressive development. The articles mentioned a few odd things like difficulty sleeping accompanied by screaming (Jillian had begun to do this) and occasional blue feet! As with Jillian's earlier neurology assessment, God gave us a few days to mull over this potential diagnosis. When we met with the doctor, who after a thorough evaluation diagnosed Jillian with Rett, we were prepared for the news. In her office, I felt the crushing pain and nausea for the second time – but I also felt God's peace.

Because Jillian was young for this diagnosis (at this time, before the genetic test, most Rett children were diagnosed as preschoolers or later), the doctor suggested we have it confirmed by a Rett specialist in Birmingham, Alabama. I remember sitting in the hotel room in Birmingham with Jillian on the floor in front of me. She could still sit for brief periods, but she soon toppled over. When she tried to move to a toy and couldn't, she cried and cried. It broke my heart to see her realize that her world was falling apart. I was observing her regression, but she was living it. When we met with the specialist, he confirmed what we feared, and once again I experienced that now-familiar reaction to tragic news: deep, immediate nausea. But Paul and I were still able to participate in a meaningful exchange of information with the doctor, instead of just sitting there in shock. I was so grateful both for the early diagnosis and for God preparing us each step of the way. As we let the diagnosis sink in, I faced a hard truth: not only was Jillian's brain injured and her normal life over, but things were going to get worse.

On returning from Birmingham, I had the oddest sensation everywhere I went: I felt like I had a neon sign over my head that said, "My child has Rett syndrome." In the grocery store checkout line, interacting with the clerk, I felt that she could read the sign and tell the agony I was in. Surely it was not business as usual. I wanted to explain to complete strangers why I was just a shell walking around. These feelings caught me off-guard, as I had never experienced devastating news and profound grief before. Trying to understand what I felt, I turned to C.S. Lewis's *A Grief Observed.* He writes:

> No one ever told me that grief felt so like fear. I am not afraid, but the sensation is like being afraid. The same fluttering in the stomach, the same restlessness, the yawning. I keep on swallowing . . . At other times it feels like being mildly drunk, or concussed. There is a sort of invisible blanket between the world and me. I find it hard to take in what anyone says. Or perhaps, hard to want to take it in. It is so uninteresting. Yet I want the others to be about me. I dread the moments when the house is empty. If only they would talk to one another and not to me.[1]

I knew I was experiencing tragedy for the first time in my life, yet I was not screaming or crying or pounding my fists. My reaction was very interior, with altered body sensations and thought. Lewis had lost his wife to a drawn-out fight with cancer. Similarly, our precious little girl was slowly deteriorating in front of us. It felt as if she was being stolen away. Lewis described my feelings in a nutshell. But this at least showed me that others had felt as I did, and I was not alone. I allowed myself to grieve as Lewis did after losing his wife. I repeated this process many times over the next several years: grieving the loss and the tragedy for Jillian and me, in order to embrace the joy in my daughter and our new life together.

Since I now had information about Jillian's condition and was learning about grief, I wanted to involve our boys, who were three and five years old. They loved their sister and went to therapy with her. They already knew something was wrong because we had told them that Jillian was not doing things other babies her age were doing. But now I sat down with them and told them about Rett syndrome and what was ahead. Even though they could not understand the full implications of Jillian's condition, they still grieved. I did not try to put a positive spin on the information, but I did tell them that I knew God was good and trusted He had a bigger plan than we could see right now. I tried to explain how hard this must be for Jillian and we cried together. They asked if she would die and if God would heal her. I tried to answer their direct questions with direct answers. I also had to say, "I don't know." Over the next several years, Paul and I continued to communicate honestly with the boys about Jillian's condition, good or bad. We always gave them the same information we had so they could participate fully in rejoicing or grieving, as the situation warranted.

From the first day of this hard journey, God used the experiences of our lives to show me He cared. These experiences were like a trail of breadcrumbs through the forest. They let me know that He saw me and saw my daughter, even if He did not heal her. Around the time of Jillian's diagnosis, for instance, God demonstrated his love and provision in the guise of a family trip. One day while throwing out his junk mail at work, Paul caught sight of a brochure for an upcoming Christian Medical Dental Association conference. It was something he would usually ignore, but he called me up and said, "I think we are supposed to go to this."

He read me the details: an all-inclusive week at a ranch in Colorado, a good speaker, programs for the kids, etc. The details were attractive, but the logistics were daunting. Still, we felt God had something for us there. Because of Jillian's sleep difficulties and our family's size, we needed a particular kind of accommodation. But when Paul called the conference center to make our reservations, all the appropriate rooms were taken. The receptionist promised to call us if anything changed, but she warned us that the center rarely had cancellations. Nevertheless, a few weeks before the conference, we got a call: there had been a cancellation, and we could have just the accommodation we needed.

I remember thinking it was a miracle—the exact thing we had asked for, something that had seemed impossible to get. I had been pounding on heaven's doors for Jillian's normal development, and this blocked path to Colorado cleared without effort. I thought, "Surely God cares more about the health of my child than what hotel room we get!" What was God trying to teach me? I decided God was showing us that He cared very much about us, and if He cared about the little things, He cared about the big things, too. If He chose not to heal Jillian, He had a good reason, and we could trust Him to show us how to walk with her. That conference was a strategic time in the life of our family. Our boys had some much-needed carefree time, and the ranch assigned a staff person to take care of Jillian. Paul and I received support from the other conference attendees, and we listened to the keynote speaker, Dr. Richard Swenson, talk about the importance of maintaining margin in our lives. We learned that this meant leaving space in our schedules to respond intentionally to life rather than simply react, and to savor life's important moments. This lesson would be invaluable on our journey with Jillian.

Looking back at Jillian's life, I can recall these key experiences that God used to teach and equip us. Like Mary, Jesus's mother, who after the shepherds' visit and finding the boy Jesus teaching in the temple "treasured up all these things and pondered them in her heart" (Luke 2:19, NIV), I stored up these incidents.

Soon after the Colorado conference, we encountered God again in Minneapolis, where we were visiting family. There, we attended Bethlehem Baptist Church, pastored by Dr. John Piper. We were excited to worship there; Paul had heard Dr. Piper speak at a conference in college, and we'd met a missionary family from Bethlehem Baptist while we were serving in Ecuador.

Dr. Piper delivered his message from two verses: Matthew 6:34 ("Therefore do not be anxious for tomorrow; for tomorrow will care for itself. Each day has enough trouble of its own") and Lamentations 3:22-23 ("The Lord's loving kindnesses indeed never cease, for his compassions never fail. They are new every morning; great is Thy faithfulness"). He began by making these observations: we try to worry, anticipate, or "feel the grace" for much in our future. We ask, "What will happen when my mother dies? How will I survive if I lose my job? What will happen if I get cancer?" But Dr. Piper's thesis was that God does not give us the grace we need until we need it—and then it comes powerfully. He said:

> … there is fresh mercy from God for each day's appointed pain. Today's mercies are not designed to carry tomorrow's burdens. There will be mercies tomorrow for that. Today's mercies are for today's burdens … What you need today is not tomorrow's strength, but today's faith that tomorrow's mercies will be new and will be enough.[2]

To illustrate his point, Piper told the powerful story of John Vinson, a missionary to the Chinese. Along with the rest of his village, Vinson was kidnapped by bandits. When Vinson refused to go free or flee because the bandits would not also free their Chinese prisoners, a bandit pointed a gun at Vinson's head and said, "I'm going to kill you. Aren't you afraid?"

Piper paused here, looked at us intently, and said:

> Now at this point how do you feel? Are you projecting yourself into Vinson's place? If so, do you feel rising within you the power to respond with great serenity and to die with peace? The point of what I have been saying is this: you don't have to feel that right now. What God wants from you now as you sit there is not the strength to die that death. That is not today's trouble for you. It may

> be tomorrow's. What God calls you to now is not to have the power to do what Vinson did, but to have the trust in God that when your time comes, he will give what you need.

Piper concluded the story and his sermon:

> Vinson looked up and said, "No, I am not afraid. If you kill me, I will go straight to God." Which he did. Today's mercies for today's troubles; tomorrow's mercies for tomorrow's troubles. "As your days so shall your strength be" (Deuteronomy 33:25). Don't be anxious about tomorrow. The troubles and the mercies are appointed day by day.

This idea of not trying to "feel the grace" in advance proved indispensable in our walk with Jillian. Many terrifying scenarios loomed on the horizon, and we did not have the grace for them today. We had to stop speculating, let go of future stress, and trust that we would have God's grace for whatever came our way. At this point, we knew that Jillian would never be a typical child. Unless God chose to touch her and remove the damaged gene from every cell in her body, her ongoing development would be abnormal. We also knew that our family, our marriage, and our lives would never be the same. But we also knew that God was on our side, and He would give each of us what we needed.

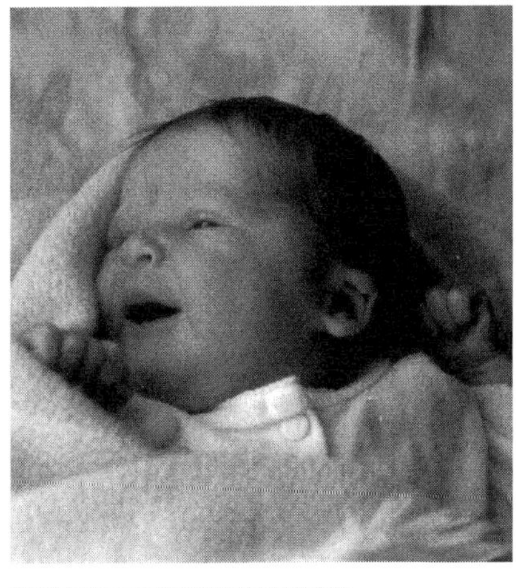

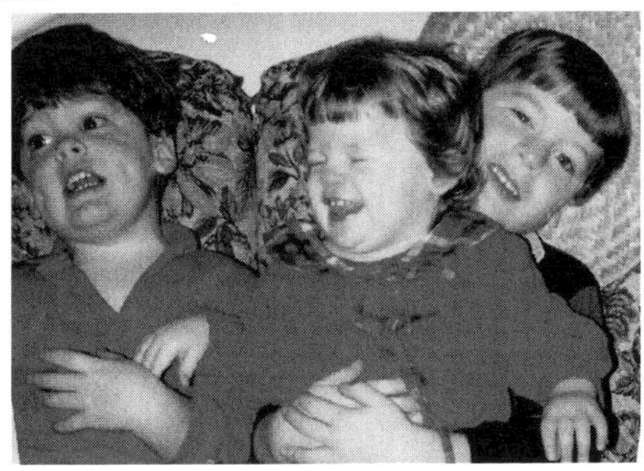

Jillian before regression: newborn through one year old. Pictured with Paul (top) and Andrew and Luke (bottom).

Jillian during regression:
detached and passive.
Pictured with Joyce.

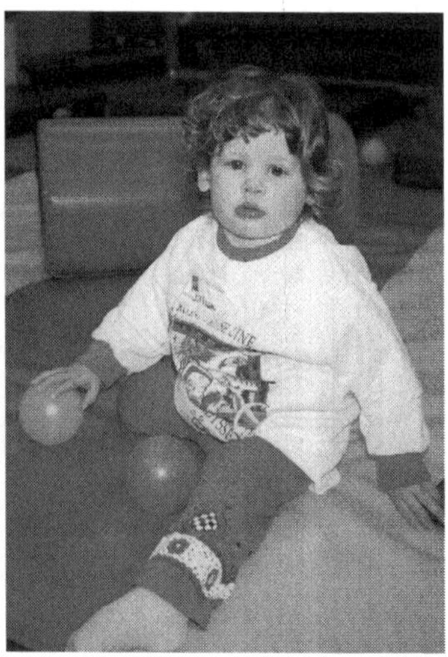

Chapter 2

Reality Sets in

Diagnosis Through Regression

If the Lord had not been on our side—
Let Israel say—
If the Lord had not been on our side
When men attacked us,
When their anger flared against us,
They would have swallowed us alive;
The flood would have engulfed us,
The torrent would have swept us away.
The raging waters
Would have swept us away.

Praise be to the Lord,
Who has not let us be torn by their teeth.
We have escaped like a bird
Out of the fowler's snare;
The snare has been broken,
And we have escaped.
Our help is in the name of the Lord,
The maker of heaven and earth.

Psalm 124 (NIV)

Once we had a diagnosis of Rett syndrome for Jillian, we could anticipate something of the road ahead. I made it my job to learn all I could. The World Wide Web was still new and fairly unreliable, so most of my information-gathering took traditional paths: books, articles, VHS tapes, and phone calls. I joined the International Rett Syndrome Association (now the International Rett Syndrome Foundation, IRSF) and through them ordered videos, medical articles, and a handbook they published. Here I saw the first pictures of other girls with Rett, from toddler to adult, and I could see what they were able to do. I learned that Rett is a spectrum disorder—some girls are affected more severely than others. I watched videos of girls working during therapy and walking haltingly after regression. I read about the stages Rett girls go through as they grow up, and how they are "locked inside" their uncooperative bodies.

One article by an educational researcher arrested my attention; it demonstrated that Rett girls wanted desperately to communicate or interact with other people and their environment but could not make their bodies act accordingly. I learned that a Rett girl's ability to think and understand is independent of her physical disability. My phone conversations with other IRSF mothers confirmed this hidden intelligence. One mom told me that her teenage daughter, having never spoken a word, suddenly spoke a single sentence, then relapsed into silence. Others told me that their girls would laugh at appropriate times in movies. These stories convinced me that Jillian was still there, riding out the storm of her body going awry, and I needed to hold on tight to her. In short, my research showed me how to understand Jillian and gave me vision for parenting her in the context of Rett syndrome.

Looking ahead, Paul and I knew Jillian would lose most of her developmental milestones over the course of her regression. We also knew the regression would end at some point. As Jillian's regression continued, her agitation increased, and she became intolerant of therapy. She also suffered from sleep disruptions, which left her exhausted and often caused her to need a nap just when it was time for therapy. We were reluctant to walk away from therapy because, as parents, we were desperate to do everything we could for Jillian. But she was suffering greatly and getting nothing out of the appointments, so we made the difficult decision to postpone therapy for a season. This decision was just one of many choices we made as we attempted to balance our family's need for normalcy with Jillian's limited tolerance for activity and her need to simply be loved through her crisis. We lived life as a family, and tried not to let Rett syndrome steal any more from us than it had to.

As Jillian grew but continued to regress, adaptive equipment became a fixture in our lives. Our first item was a corner chair with a tray table. It supported Jillian's body while she played in a sitting position, and it had wheels so we could move her around the house. When we acquired the chair, Jillian still had some use of her hands, and she often tried to play with the items on her tray. I especially remember a time when my parents came to visit, and Jillian was sitting in this chair. On the tray in front of her was a wooden switch with a large, bright plastic button. A wire ran from the switch to the floor, where it connected to a battery-operated Cookie Monster pushing a cart of cookies. Jillian looked so apathetic and passive sitting there. But then she suddenly flung her arm onto the tray and pushed the switch. She turned to watch the toy move noisily across the floor. My parents stood watching in shock; Jillian understood cause and effect!

We also had a stander, which was a wooden board with straps and a tray. We would lay Jillian on the board and strap her into a standing position, then push the board upright and attach the tray. Children need to bear weight on their legs as they grow to promote regular bone growth. The stander was designed to help Jillian play contentedly in an upright position, but as she grew fussier, she had little tolerance for the stander. We were not able to use it regularly until later, after she stopped regressing. Other adaptive equipment included a waterbed, which helped her sleep because it was heated and conformed to her body, and braces to help straighten and strengthen her legs and torso. And of course there was a wheelchair that had straps to keep her upright, but she wrestled against it most of the time. In fact, Jillian fought against most of the equipment, as it only increased her anger, discomfort, fatigue, and confusion. Every time we got something new, I had a moment of hope, thinking of ways the equipment would help Jillian, but most things turned out to be a disappointment. In the end, we simply had to get through regression and see what the storm left in its wake.

I made the following notes in Jillian's journal about her disappearing developmental milestones:

1995: A year of loss, learning, and love

crawl—gone	laugh—gone
clap—gone	sit—gone
play—gone	curls—gone
smile—gone	grasp—gone

The rest of the entry is a stream-of-consciousness paragraph, tracing the circles my thoughts seemed to follow every day:

> Read—cry—read, Rett syndrome, information, videos, therapists, doctors, specialists, genetics, early intervention, God is in control, hope, healing, prayer, comfort, Surely the arm of the Lord is not too short to save … tests, x-rays, corner chair, stander, wheelchair, swing, waterbed, brace

I concluded with this list of what we had lost for her future:

> Jillian:
> Her voice, her growing body, her childhood, her movements: hugs, walking, dancing, clapping, running, skipping, arms up
>
> Her health, her friendships, her play, her passions, her desires, her thoughts about God, her song, her independence, her ideas, her expressions, her growing up, her marrying, children, work, her obvious affection, her mind, her creativity
>
> Everything is so hard: eating, sleeping, transporting, sitting, discerning needs, communicating

Jillian's season of regression was the darkest time of my life. Like most people, I was afraid of darkness. I was afraid of the unknown, of pain, of suffering, of loss of control, of death. I had never experienced much suffering. Raised in a loving home, I always had everything I needed. I attended a good college, traveled overseas, and married my first love. I had a relationship with God and felt loved by Him. I was a mother at home, the role I'd always wanted. But now I found myself in a dark, truly miserable place. While I grieved over Jillian's condition, I had the additional challenge of managing her daily care. Sleep (or, rather, lack thereof) was one of the most difficult aspects of Jillian's care, both for me and for her. Jillian could not put herself to sleep. She screamed every night, sometimes for hours. I could nurse her to sleep, but if I moved, she woke up. She never cried herself to sleep; she just kept crying. And it was an agonizing cry. It was not sad or angry. It was painful and desperate and tortured. Since Paul had to go to work each morning, I spent most nights with Jillian. Even if he volunteered to stay up with her (and he often did), I lay awake and listened to her scream. Sleeping medicines only made her lethargic the next day. Our only respite was a children's music video called *Five Little Ladybugs*, which she would watch over and over, quiet in our arms. Five hours of sleep—for me or for her —was something to celebrate.

Psalm 127:2 says, "He grants sleep to those he loves" (NIV). I knew God loved Jillian and me, so I recited that promise and prayed that God would put Jillian to sleep. Nothing changed. One night I was up again, exhausted and angry. I was not angry with God that Jillian had Rett syndrome, but I was angry that Jillian could not sleep! I yelled out in the night to God, with Jillian screaming in my arms: "What are you going to do? *Why* are you not fixing this?" And inside I heard a quiet answer: "You are praying the wrong prayer." It stopped me mid-sob. What was the right prayer?

The next night, I prayed, "God, please give me what I need to take care of Jillian tonight. Keep my family asleep and rest them. Give me the sleep I need and keep me from freaking out if my night of sleep is short. Give me strength and joy to take care of Luke and Andrew tomorrow." And God answered that prayer.

Day after day, I had what I needed. At night, I had what I needed. It was still hard at times, and I still got mad. But those nighttime sessions with Jillian became the bedrock of our relationship. She learned to receive comfort from me, and I learned to help her. We had many sweet hours balled up together in her bed. Instead of fighting the situation, I learned to pray through the many hours I lay awake.

Jillian's regression lasted almost two years. Some days, she seemed to progress, but then she would lose more ground. She stopped feeding herself and using her hands. She stopped moving voluntarily. For me, the most devastating loss was her eye contact. She stopped looking at us and responding and smiling. She stopped vocalizing, except for crying at night. She always had a far away look on her face and seemed distracted and detached. Despite this fading ability to participate and interact, we continued to take her everywhere with us. She was a gentle child with beautiful auburn curls, so people responded well to her in public.

God took care of us in our suffering, giving us what we needed as the months unfolded. All our relatives lived far away, so our church became our family. They prayed for us, brought us meals, and babysat our boys. They welcomed Jillian and treated her with kindness, talking to her or holding her.

One day, I asked a church friend if I should be doing more to help Jillian—more praying or fasting—and she answered, "You just push the wheelchair." God was telling me through my friend to leave the prayer and fasting to our church body as I had my hands full with Jillian's daily care. I am so grateful for our community, as they provided a tangible sign of God's attention. Even though Jillian could not have a typical childhood, she could have a life rich in love, friendship, and extended family. One of the many losses when you have a special needs child is the typical birthday party, but I needed to have a party to celebrate Jillian. We decided to have an open house, invite those who had walked closely with us through regression, and call it a Bring-a-Bib Birthday Bash. With plenty of good food and a crowd of people coming and going, I felt happy and energized. It served as a great deposit of hope. I still have some of the bibs.

Another time, God reached out to me when I was attending a conference. During a time of prayer, I got a mental picture of myself walking down a road with Jesus. He was smiling, carrying Jillian on His shoulder, and had His hand extended toward mine, inviting me to go along with them. I noticed that the road turned ahead, so I could not see the destination. I felt like Jesus was asking me to walk with Him on this journey while He carried Jillian. I chose to go with Him that night. Over the years that followed, I could sometimes tell when I had pulled Jillian off Jesus' shoulders and was trying to carry her myself. Those were the times when I felt like I was dying under the load. But as long as I let Him carry her, the journey was bearable.

As our family walked through Jillian's regression, we also started to learn more universal things about people with disabilities: their struggles, achievements, and gifts. Slowly we began to gain some perspective on Jillian's condition and her suffering, and on what she could teach those of us who were caught in an over-productive, performance-based lifestyle. Our first encounter with this material came from a sidebar in my study bible: a Max Lucado excerpt:

> In my closet hangs a sweater that I seldom wear. It is too small. The sleeves are too short, the shoulders too tight. Some of the buttons are missing, and the thread is

> frazzled. I should throw that sweater away. I have no use for it. I'll never wear it again. Logic says I should clear out the space and get rid of the sweater.
>
> That's what logic says.
>
> But love won't let me.[1]

Lucado goes on to explain that the sweater was not store-bought, but made by his mother, who crafted it with intentionality, effort, and affection. He concludes, "And though the sweater has lost all of its use, it has lost none of its value. It is valuable not because of its function, but because of its maker." Intellectually we know we have value because God made us and loves us, but the world constantly lifts up performance and accomplishment as the measure of human worth. Jillian became that sweater in our family, reminding us of our true worth. Later, Paul read the story at a gathering of parents of children with special needs, and at Jillian's funeral.

Slowly we began to embrace Jillian's different life and the possibilities—not just hindrances—that lay before us. This last letter I wrote to Jillian summarizes my feelings during her regression. (I didn't know it would be my last, but it became too painful to write to her, knowing she would never read my letters.)

> It has been a year since I've written in your book. And what a year! I had no idea last January what lay ahead. We watched our precious angel slowly gain a few skills and then lose them. It was so insidious that several months went by before we realized what was going on: you were regressing. God was faithful to show us each turn on the path, but the path was rocky and hard.

Suddenly a remote and unlikely diagnosis became reality: Rett syndrome. All the details of this year I hope to write somewhere else, and perhaps it can help someone else someday. But where are we now, in 1996? Well, we had a wonderful birthday for you on Nov. 19 with most of your and our friends there. It was a celebration of you and your Maker, not what you can do. Then Dec. was a hard month, with much fussing and illness and poor sleep. I realized I needed help, and God provided someone to come every morning. And then over Christmas and New Year's, it just seemed you were doing better. Better eye contact, more interest in your environment, and a smile! The first we'd seen in months. What does this mean? Have you come to the end of this regression phase? Today you are sick with a cold or flu.

I am confident only in God's control of this situation and that if we let Him, He will use you to change us dramatically. You bless many with just your sweetness. On Christmas Eve we attended church with Aunt Linda, Uncle Ed, and Grandma, and you sat so content with your Dad. We so much want you back. But you still bless us with your soft skin, beautiful face and hair, peaceful sighs and closeness. I cut your hair one night this fall and cried so hard. Your baby curls are gone, but your hair is still lovely.

So now we are turning a corner. I have a sense of expectation, although I know things will be challenging. And I pray for you, Jillian, as you get further trapped by your physical body, that you will sense the Holy Spirit in your innermost being, that He will comfort you, and fill you with hope in your God.

> We're in this together, kid! May 1996 bring glory to God in both of our lives.

From the beginning of my marriage, I had taken full responsibility for cleaning, cooking, and laundry. But now Jillian was taking more time, and I still had young boys. I asked the director of our church nursery if she knew anyone who could help me with Jillian. She recommended Kristina, a homeschooled teenager, and Kristina began caring for Jillian during the day. She sat with Jillian or took her for walks while I went to the grocery store or cleaned the house. Mary Britton was a student majoring in special education at Vanderbilt. She also spent time working with Jillian. Later on Christine, a mother with grown children, came two days a week to clean for us; eventually, she learned to take care of Jillian too. Christine worked with Jillian for the rest of Jillian's life. Thus began one of the best parts of our journey with Jillian: walking with the people God raised up to help us care for her. Throughout her life, various nurses, young people, special education students, mothers, and more would come into our home to spend time with her.

For example, when Jillian was about three, we attended a Christmas party where an acquaintance of ours, Jane Carroll, asked if she could hold Jillian while we got something to eat. Jane ended up holding Jillian for most of the evening. Several days later, she called me and said, "I know this sounds strange, but I would like to give you a break one morning a week and hold Jillian while I homeschool my kids. I want to spend time with Jillian." So for two years I drove to Jane's home once a week so Jillian could sit in Jane's arms. I usually spent the time walking at a nearby lake. Since I enjoy nature and connect well with God in that context, those walks brought me sanity. I prayed, cried, thought, and let creation minister to me.

Jane and other women like her didn't just take care of Jillian. They also gave something to me: breathing room, time to get away and be alone with God or with my boys or my husband or a friend. These women lightened my load and helped me grieve and laugh along the way. What started as a necessity for me became a gift for Jillian and ultimately for our family. A common challenge of parenting a child with special needs is being resistant to seeking out or even accepting help from others. You know your child better than anyone, and so many things can go wrong. But I believe our family and Jillian herself would have suffered if I had not accepted help. I had to give up control. I had to let Jesus carry Jillian through these women. I realized that I could either drive myself crazy trying to anticipate everything that could happen, or I could simply choose to trust that God would take care of us if something happened to Jillian while I was away. Eventually, I even learned to leave Jillian in others' care overnight. These caregivers primarily had relationship with her, as opposed to being my friend who took care of my child. They were Jillian's friends. I am so glad I allowed people to care for her physically, as that was the only way to get close to her. *

At the end of Jillian's regression, when the boys were five and seven, we decided to go to Ecuador one more time. Because we had been to the same place three times before, we could jump right into the community, and Paul could function independently in the hospital. Jillian was still small enough to be carried in our arms, and an Ecuadorian woman agreed to help me take care of

---

* Please see the Afterword for collected reflections from Jillian's main caregivers.

her there. Still, the plane trip would be long and our boys needed attention as well as Jillian. We heard from our missionary friends in Ecuador that a high school girl from Nashville planned on visiting them. We met her, and she agreed to travel with us and help look after the boys on the way. This girl's parents saw us as provision for their daughter's international travel, and we saw her as a gift from God. We felt called to go back to Ecuador in spite of our hard circumstances, and God opened a clear path for us to go. So we made the trip to Quito through Miami. Then we got on a six-seat Cessna and flew to Shell on the edge of the rainforest. Jillian was more stable now; her eye contact was better, and she traveled well. While she remained fussy at night, she was easier to calm. We stayed in Ecuador a month, and the trip taught us that we could still do things as a family with Jillian. The trip also showed us that Jillian had her own ministry to everyone she met. She was not some heavy baggage that we had to cart around in order to do what we wanted. Now that her disabilities were more obvious, she was beginning to have an impact on those she encountered at airports, restaurants, and stores. From the Ecuadorian woman who babysat her to the missionary community where we served—and even to complete strangers along the way—Jillian touched people with her quiet, peaceful presence. We were her ambassadors. We simply had to push the wheelchair.

Two moments from that trip stand out in my memory. One night early in the trip, I was able to get Jillian to sleep at a reasonable time—and here we were on the edge of the rainforest! I felt pretty proud of myself. I was cleaning up the kitchen, and Paul was with me. As I worked happily, full of hope that life was looking up, I put on a CD and a song about being in love began to play. I said something lighthearted to Paul about the song, and he replied bluntly, "I feel like you have another man in your life, and his name is Rett syndrome." I was shocked. Then I was disheartened, then scared. Hadn't I been doing my best? Wasn't I coping well? Wasn't God carrying us?

Paul and I began to discuss what he was feeling. I realized that I had become so concerned with learning about Rett and taking care of Jillian and our boys that he felt ignored. To make matters worse, since he is a pediatrician, I tended to pepper him with questions and anxieties about Jillian during his free time. In short, Jillian's condition had consumed me. After our conversation, I was grieved but also thankful that he had told me his feelings. I knew that 80 percent of marriages with a child who has special needs end in divorce. I did not want to head into that statistic with bravado; we would have to act deliberately if we wanted our marriage and family to thrive. That night, Paul and I prayed, I apologized, and we vowed to keep the discussion going. We asked God for His protection over our marriage and for His help, acknowledging that our relationship would fail without His support.

My second memory is from the end of our month in Shell. Instead of flying back to Quito, we drove back in a van with some missionary friends. The drive took all day because of road conditions: the main road had partially washed away, so we had to drive over bumpy, unpaved back roads. As we climbed the Andes, our friends decided to take us to a mountaintop village called Papallacta, which is known for its hot springs. Late in the afternoon, we pulled into a resort filled with Ecuadorians swimming in several large, rock-rimmed pools. Since we were at a high elevation near nightfall, it was freezing outside. Paul took the boys into one rudimentary changing stall, while I took Jillian into another. She got cold very quickly, and there was no good place to lay her down. The wind blew fiercely as I battled to get a swimsuit on her somewhat limp body. Then I scooped her up and ran to the pool. Thankfully, it was quite warm. Jillian loved to be held in water, especially in warm water. As I stepped into the water with her, she immediately stopped shivering and relaxed. Soon, a few giggles escaped from her happy body. I held her and looked around. We were at the top of a mountain in South America, surrounded by local people who had received us all—including Jillian—with the utmost kindness. Higher peaks surrounded us, the air was crisp, and a beautiful moon shone through the trees. Our boys were splashing and having fun. I was so grateful to be there with our whole family. Surely God was good and had a good plan for us, even in the setting of Jillian's brokenness.

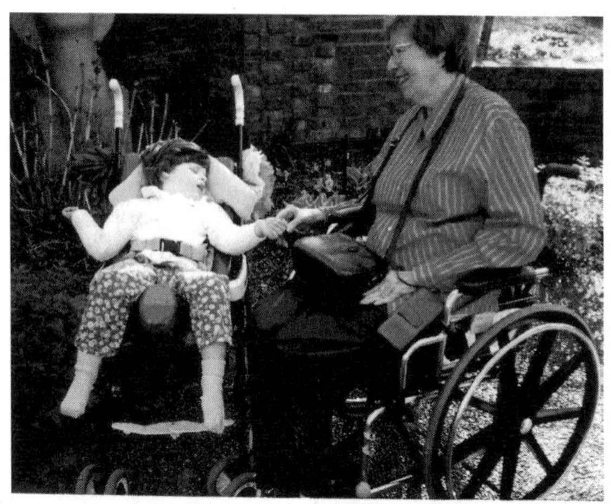

After regression: with her Grandma, a caregiver in Ecuador, in her adaptive chair with Paul, and with the boys.

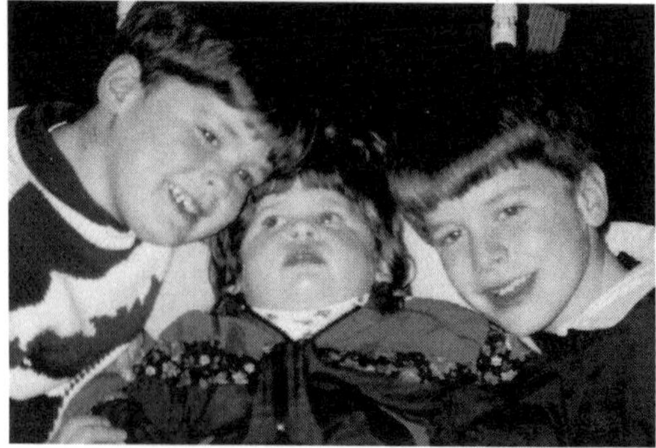

Chapter 3

The Calm Between Storms

Age 3 through 6

Somewhere between the fact of darkness and the hope of light.
That is who we are.

Frederick Beuchner

Now that Jillian was through regression, she slowly regained some of her personality. Her sleep improved, and she began to make fleeting eye contact. She smiled and laughed more frequently. The next few years were like digging out from a blizzard or returning to a flooded home. We began picking up the pieces of our lives and figuring out where we were. We hired enough caregivers to give me time to breathe, read, process, walk with friends, and spend time with my boys. Slowly, God began to heal the huge wound in my soul and teach me about suffering. I realized that not only did I need to recover from the storm of Jillian's regression, but I also needed tools to walk out the changes and challenges that were yet to come. I needed to celebrate Jillian's life and spirit, but I also needed to grieve our losses. [I will share in the next chapter what I learned during this time about suffering. First, I will describe some of the stories from this part of her life that centered on her education; her health and development; and her role in our family and community.]

With regression behind us, we had space to consider Jillian's education. Many educational resources now exist for children with special needs, but for a newcomer, the process seemed overwhelming. Since her diagnosis Jillian had received therapy in our home through the Tennessee Early Intervention System. When a child turns three, the program stops providing services at home and instead provides them at the child's preschool, whether public or private. So now that Jillian was three, it was time to choose her preschool. We started by developing an Individual Education Plan (IEP) with the help of educators and therapists who had previously evaluated Jillian. They made recommendations and listened to what we felt Jillian needed most. Because Rett syndrome is more of a motor disability than a cognitive one, we wanted Jillian to be mainstreamed with typical children. As a pediatrician, Paul had experience intersecting with educational systems for children with special needs. He and I could talk about our goals and concerns, and then I could go to meetings equipped with our desires. If he had not been so familiar with the system and process, he would have needed to attend those meetings and visit schools. For me, it was a steep learning curve, but the school system educators worked hard to understand Jillian and hear my perspective on her disability.

I visited a few classrooms. One had both typical children and those with special needs. It was an energetic place with a lot going on, but it did not have a high staff-to-student ratio. Since Jillian could not communicate, defend herself, or move, I was nervous about leaving her relatively unattended. I also visited Harris Hillman, a school for children with multiple disabilities. The on-site resources at this amazing school were (and still are) unmatched in the area. But I remained unwilling to give up on regular preschool. Jillian's brothers had attended a local preschool at a Baptist church a few mornings a week. This nurturing environment near our home had a good curriculum and excellent teachers. With enthusiastic permission from the director, Jillian started attending class two mornings a week with an assistant provided by the school district. The teachers welcomed Jillian, and the other three-year-olds were interested in her, uninhibited, and ready to play. She attended there until kindergarten. Debbie DeSchutle worked as one of Jillian's assistants at preschool during this time. After Jillian's death, she said this in a card to us: "Jillian taught me a lot about the Lord during that short time that I watched her. She taught me some about the importance of just being in the presence of the Lord. And she was so strategic in the lives of those kids in the preschool." I remain so grateful to this preschool for welcoming our daughter as they had our sons. Later, Rachel also attended the school, and when Jillian died, Rachel's class and all the staff who had walked with us for over a decade, supported us in our grief. God did not heal Jillian, but He generously gave us community to surround us throughout her life.

Another example of community came through our sons' peers. Paul and I led a Cub Scout group in our home with Jillian in the midst of it. The Scouts behaved respectfully to her and always said hello. They got used to her coughing or drooling or leaning to one side. One time, they were eating a snack in our front yard. Jillian was parked in her wheelchair a few feet away. As the boys ate, they were talking about someone they all knew at school. Suddenly, one of them said something like, "He is so retarded!" I said, "Hey guys, is there someone in our group who could really be called retarded? Is it a kind thing to say?" I believe those boys did not think of Jillian as "retarded." They didn't even consider what the word meant when they said it. But they thought about it that day. As she did with the scouts, Jillian continually challenged our conception of what was normal or fair. When Luke or Andrew had a new friend over, they had to explain Jillian's condition to that friend. Jillian might be sitting quietly in her chair or she might even be having a small seizure, and they would still say hello and introduce their friends. Later, when Jillian died, most of those Cub Scouts and many of the boys' other friends from those years came to her funeral; several spoke at her graveside about how she had impacted their lives.

We had community within our family, too. Whatever we did during this season, Jillian participated as best she could. Sometimes, this led to awkward situations, like one summer day when I took Jillian and her brothers crayfish hunting at our neighborhood creek. When the boys were small, we spent much time at this creek, which always had its fair share of water snakes, toads, tadpoles, bullfrogs, salamanders, turtles, crayfish, and minnows. Unless a caregiver was with Jillian, she always came along on these little explorations. She liked listening to us from her chair, and we showed her our finds.

One day I put her in a special molded foam seat inserted in a stroller. It was more "all terrain" than her wheelchair, and did not constrain her with straps, letting her experience some freedom. Since she had very poor muscle tone, she did not move much. She just lay there, leaning back slightly, looking at the horizon, or occasionally pulling her head down to look in front of her. So I parked her, made sure the sun was not in her face, and started walking with the boys along the creek. Close to where she sat, a road crossed by a bridge over the creek. We wandered under the bridge because crayfish lived in the deeper, darker waters. We came out the other side, still hunting in the water. Occasionally, I peeked back under the bridge to check on Jillian. She was fine, so we stayed there looking in the water. I was vaguely conscious that a car had gone over the bridge—they came by periodically. But then I became aware of concerned voices, and I realized the car had stopped. I peered under the bridge at Jillian on the other side. She had leaned way over in the stroller; she did this regularly with perfect safety. But the stranger only saw a limp child, hanging virtually unmoving out of the side of her stroller, with no one in sight. The people from the car started to come to her aid. I quickly ran out from under the bridge and called, "Everything is all right! I'm with her. She does this all the time." I think they thought I was crazy, or at least a very bad parent. Experiences like these kept us lighthearted; sometimes, we just had to laugh at our odd life!

And while I needed to be vigilant for Jillian's safety, I also had to let her be a kid with her brothers out on a sunny afternoon.

Each new stage or event provided a new parenting challenge, walking in this tension of taking care of Jillian appropriately while still allowing her to be a child. For example, we wanted Jillian to have regular birthday parties. But what kind of birthday party do you give for a child who cannot play with toys, eat birthday cake, or talk to her guests? Jillian loved music and came alive when she heard it, so on her fifth birthday, we had a musical party. Our dear friends Chris and Leslie Norton brought their instruments to our home, and we turned our spacious entryway into a concert hall. Chris, a virtuoso marimba player, carted over his huge instrument. Leslie, the principal horn player for the Nashville Symphony, brought her French horn and an alpenhorn, which she had to play standing on a ladder! We invited friends and their children and served a menu Jillian could eat: soup, bread, and cheesecake. In lieu of gifts, guests made donations to the International Rett Syndrome Association. Jillian sat front-and-center for the concert, with the huge sounds of marimba and horn filling our home. Events like this not only helped soothe the loss of typical childhood and parenting experiences—they also made memories to enjoy later.

A month after this fifth birthday party, we discovered I was pregnant. We received the news with great joy. I had always wanted four children, and yet after Jillian I was unsure that I had the resources to take care of another. But now that Jillian was fairly stable and the boys were older, it seemed manageable. My pregnancy went well, and I had little anxiety. We found out the baby was a girl, and again my rational brain was not anxious. Rett syndrome is a random genetic event, meaning that unless the mother is a carrier, each baby has the same risk as the general population (1 in 10,000) of developing Rett syndrome. I felt sure I was not a carrier because my other pregnancies were normal, and I thought I had peace. But close to the due date, we needed to come up with a name, and I could not think of one. This seemed odd to me, so I prayed and tried to figure out why this was so hard. I realized that I had a deep desire not to be hurt by the outcome of this pregnancy, so to protect myself mentally and emotionally, I had spent little time dreaming about the new baby or anticipating her birth. Although I had succeeded at not panicking, I had not allowed myself to hope. Ultimately, our baby girl arrived easily and happily, but still we had no name! It took us about a week of holding her and letting the reality of her soak into us to settle on "Rachel." I thought all was well after that—we had passed the milestone of receiving a child. I enjoyed Rachel as she grew, and she brought life to everyone, including Jillian. It was even easier than I had expected to look after the newborn Rachel because the caregivers I had for Jillian helped with Rachel as needed.

As Rachel approached six months, however, I became more anxious. She was not rolling over yet. Paul would come home from work and say encouragingly, "I saw four six-month-olds today for their physicals, and half were not rolling over yet." Still I worried, and it was an irrational kind of worry that gripped my heart with fear. This internal stress continued until Rachel was about a year old and passed the point where Jillian had begun to regress—when she could crawl well, pull up, and then walk. It is hard to try again when you have been hurt. This early period of Rachel's development brought fear, because it was based on "what ifs" and not on actual circumstances. I remembered then something I had read in the book *Hinds Feet on High Places*. The main character, Much Afraid, has to pass through the Forests of Danger and Tribulation. She fearfully imagines all that she might encounter ahead. The Shepherd (Jesus) pleads with her to stop, saying, "...when you get to the places you dread you will find that they are as different as possible from what you have imagined, ...and if you ever let Craven Fear [Satan] begin painting a picture on the screen of your imagination, you will walk with fear and trembling and agony, where no fear is."[1] Similarly, I realized that I had experienced true tragedy in Jillian's regression and diagnosis. This panicky, drowning worry I felt for Rachel was not what true tragedy felt like. It was a counterfeit sent to immobilize and rob me. Throughout our life with Jillian, we learned that reality is sometimes bad, but fear of things that might be is much worse because it robs us of God's peace.

Each of our children, including Rachel when she was born, played a special role in helping our family to function. Luke, our oldest, was eventually strong enough to lift Jillian's 75-pound body out of her wheelchair and into bed. He also tube-fed her, by attaching a tube and large open syringe to her G-tube and pouring formula into the syringe. Andrew, for his part, was Jillian's guardian. He always kept an eye on her and let me know if she seemed uncomfortable. He loved to race down the street, pushing Jillian's chair as she laughed out loud. And both boys helped babysit. One Christmas we left Paul's mom, then 83, our two teenage boys, our handicapped daughter and our two-year-old at home together while we went to Paul's office party! We were perfectly comfortable doing this because the boys were some of Jillian's best caretakers. They knew her subtle cues. All through childhood, they were comfortable going to therapies with me and Jillian, getting me things I needed, wiping Jillian's mouth, lifting her head, adjusting her posture, and getting her into and out of the van. As Rachel grew, she played in bed with Jillian, brought her toys, and sang and talked to her. As a toddler, Rachel sat on Jillian's lap on her wheelchair. Jillian loved having Rachel near and responded to her energy. Later, during Jillian's second regression, I wanted her to be released from suffering to be happy and whole with Jesus. Then I realized that, if Jillian died so young, Rachel would not know her. So I prayed that God would allow Jillian to live long enough for Rachel to remember her. That is what happened.

One of the challenges of living with chronic suffering is to avoid allowing that suffering to dictate the parameters of your life. On the one hand, you have to be realistic and not do things that make your circumstances worse. On the other hand, you don't want to let the tragedy take more from your life than it already has. Jillian was first of all a daughter and a sister, and we were a family that needed to have common experiences together. We needed to get over the hump of extra work, hassle, and inconvenience and come up with creative ways to normalize our family experiences. Paul and I grew up traveling and wanted to travel as a family. We discovered through our involvement with Cub Scouts that Jillian liked to camp, so we became a camping family. We planned ahead for an annual Memorial Day camping trip so that the opportunity would not just slip by, consumed by the chaos of daily life. On our trips, Jillian and I slept in the foldout backseat bed of our conversion van while the rest of the family slept in a tent. This way, her sleeplessness did not disturb the others, and vice versa. Paul usually went hiking with the boys while I strolled with Jillian through the campgrounds or on paved trails. We usually camped near a lake and all went swimming together. As I remember these times, Jillian's disability is not a primary character in our family story.

We also took some long-distance trips. Once we flew to Arizona and rented a van with a lift. After visiting Paul's sister and her husband and exploring mines, ghost towns, and Native American ruins, we drove to the Grand Canyon. We had an accessible room on the edge of the canyon and discovered a paved walkway along the rim. So while Paul and the boys hiked down to the canyon floor and camped, Jillian, 18-month-old Rachel, and I strolled the rim, took in the gorgeous vista, and explored the area. I felt excited that we could do this, and Jillian seemed alert and attentive to everything around her. Yes, she had screamed before she got to sleep—I prayed the guests in the next room would not think we were beating her. Yes, it was hard changing Jillian's diaper on the airplane—Paul and I had to lay her down on the bulkhead floor to get the job done. But we had been to the Grand Canyon! We used to say that Jillian "just liked to be along," and she was certainly at her happiest when she was in the thick of our family activity.

As Jillian got bigger, containing her on a plane proved challenging, and we began to feel self-conscious about disturbing those around us. Around town, transferring Jillian from her wheelchair to an ill-fitting car seat and then hefting the wheelchair into the trunk of our minivan became more and more difficult. We needed a vehicle that could carry Jillian *in* her wheelchair, so we purchased a full-size conversion van with an undercarriage-mounted lift. Our boys said we were the only ones with an elevator in our car. They proudly showed it off to their friends. We'd lower the lift with a controller, wheel Jillian on backwards, and then raise the lift. At the top, we'd pull her chair into the van (carefully, so as not to hit her head on the doorframe), and we'd tie all four wheels down with special anchors. We had very comfy seats (one taken out so the wheelchair could be strapped down) and a TV/VCR/Nintendo 64 combo system. I felt like I was driving a living room down the highway! This became our main way to travel across the country, and our boys looked forward to those big car trips.

Even with the best-laid plans, however, traveling with Jillian could be hard. One day, I had the van all loaded with suitcases and was picking up the boys from school to head to Florida. I waited in the carpool area and the boys dashed excitedly to the van. I loaded up their stuff and then realized that Jillian had had a large bowel movement. I could not start the trip with her in a dirty diaper, so right there I got her out of her chair and changed her in the van. The smell was bad, and I had to change all her clothes. We didn't want anyone to see what I was doing; vacation should not start this way! Although I was frustrated by the mess and by working in a tight space, I kept a fairly positive attitude and told the boys that in the big picture of our break, this was a small event. Soon it was over, Jillian was settled, and we were off. The boys were better for it all because it helped teach them that life is messy (literally as well as figuratively!), and it is not all about us and our expectations. We could not be angry at Jillian; time and again we needed to extend beyond our usual resources to serve her. Our attitudes were the only thing we could control, so we did our best to keep them positive.

On our road trips, we drove to Colorado, Michigan, Sanibel Island, Florida, Toronto, and multiple times to Pittsburgh, and Iowa (where our parents lived) We had great family vacations. We took Jillian to the headwaters of the Colorado River, where there is a handicapped trail. We took her to the top of Clingman's Dome in the Smoky Mountains. We dragged her beanbag chair onto the beach so she could sit with us all. We pushed her and her chair through multiple theme parks. In fact, the boys always told people that one of the things Jillian brought to our family was the ability to skip lines at Disney. We took her on Pirates of the Caribbean (but not Space Mountain). We went to waterparks, aquariums, museums, and historic sites. We divided and conquered when necessary, but it is amazing what you can do with a wheelchair these days. We got to do as much as any family. And everywhere we went, we pushed Jillian, and she brought out the best in us and in those around us.

Because children with special needs often look different, their parents sometimes find it hard to be out in public. We were fortunate in that Jillian was fairly typical-looking, except that she was in a wheelchair. Most people just thought she was sleepy. She was also non-verbal her whole life, so she did not make odd or attention-getting noises. At this stage, she did not even cry much during the day. She was peaceful, and strangers liked to comment on her pretty red hair. Some siblings have to contend with strangers staring while their sister or brother with special needs attempts to communicate or use their uncooperative body. Jillian did drool, but we kept up with it. So we went everywhere, and most of the time I did not find it uncomfortable. People usually went out of their way to help us. They smiled, said a kind word, or held open a door.

Children were the most curious, and they often asked their mothers loud questions: "Why is that girl not moving? Why is she in a chair? Can she walk? Is that girl asleep?" When the parents would try to hush the children or move to the next aisle of the store, I would just answer the questions: "Part of her brain is broken, and she can't tell her body what to do. She wants to look at you and smile, but she can't. If you look closely, she will glance at you quickly. You ask good questions. She doesn't mind our talking about it." This usually turned an awkward moment into a pleasant exchange. I do not want to say that it was always easy being in public or that I did not feel grief—I did. Being with someone with special needs always draws attention. You are never anonymous. You are always different. But if given the chance, Jillian connected with passersby. She desensitized people to the "weirdness" of her situation, and most people adapted quickly to having her around. Occasionally people would say something awkward or insensitive, or perhaps they would stare. I soon came to realize this was about them, not about me, and if I responded with a smile and acted like it was ordinary for someone to be out and about in a wheelchair, they usually came around. More often, people who had a child like Jillian would talk to us, so we made friends along the way. Taking Jillian around town to parks, her brothers' activities, the mall, and restaurants not only allowed her to experience those things but added normalcy to our lives.

Even though Jillian was more stable overall during this period, her medical symptoms continued to progress and deteriorate. One morning when Jillian was three, we woke to find her in status epilepticus—experiencing seizures that wouldn't stop. This was her first experience with seizures. We had been praying that she would not get them, but here they were. After a hospitalization, we got her on medicines that mostly kept the seizures at bay. Around this same time, Jillian's eating became more challenging, and it seemed she was vomiting up her food with every meal. I found it frustrating to slowly get a jar of baby food into her, then see her gag and bring it all back up again. She was thin, and mealtimes were unpleasant. Our Rett specialist in Alabama, Dr. Alan Percy, suggested we get a surgically placed feeding tube, also known as a G-tube. A G-tube goes from the outer abdomen through to the stomach. A button rests on the tummy enabling a caregiver to attach a tube with liquid or pureed foods at mealtimes. Some children receive formula at night in a continuous feed pumped slowly into the tube. This seemed like another loss for Jillian, and I felt like I was giving up on her. I wanted her to be able to experience normal eating as one of life's pleasures, so I fought the idea. According to Dr. Percy, however, his patients' parents never regretted the decision—in fact, most wished they had done it sooner.

I decided to listen to the collective wisdom. Jillian had G-tube surgery and a fundoplication, a procedure that would prevent her from throwing up so often. In the hospital, I had my nursing baby Rachel in one bed and my five-year-old Jillian in the other. It seemed so crazy, but we all did well. Friends, hospital workers, and doctors worked hard to take care of us. Afterwards, I still gave Jillian bites of food by mouth on occasion; however, she tended to cough and choke, which put her at risk for aspiration (sucking food particles or liquid into her lungs, which can then become infected). Because she did not chew, her teeth did not erupt through her gums correctly. So she underwent dental surgery to release her teeth to the surface, only for us to discover that they had developed with cavities already in them. This led to much dental work, fortunately provided by a special-needs-certified dentist. Her new G-tube served her well, and she gained weight. Mealtimes were no longer a battle, and I could even give her bad-tasting medicines through the tube. And after all the dental work, her teeth looked natural when she smiled.

God indeed gave us the grace to walk out every hard situation during this phase of Jillian's life. When I remember her hospitalizations and surgeries, most of the memories are positive. In fact, throughout Jillian's life, we received excellent healthcare from many professionals. Most treated Jillian as a regular person and addressed her as well as me when they entered the room. Most respected my input and listened to my concerns. Most were able to acknowledge their limits when we ran into dead ends with her care. In turn, I learned to be a good medical advocate. Since Jillian could not speak for herself, I had to be with her and monitor everything that happened in a hospital setting. Thankfully, most physicians are not threatened by parent-advocates. Instead they appreciate collaboration. They realize how complicated medicine has become and that, often, the parent is the best authority on their child. As with any functional working relationship, I had to be a clear communicator: asking questions, expressing concerns, and saying no to a recommendation if I felt it would not serve Jillian. It's easy to forget that as patients, we are the consumer, and we have the right to stay engaged in the medical process until we get what we need. I also desired to be positive and thankful, remembering that every professional who took care of us was trying their best to meet our needs. Taking offense or jumping to conclusions about motives only led to anxiety for me. I tried to remind myself that if I ever had a question or disagreement about something that was going to be done to Jillian—a blood test that seemed unnecessary or a medicine I didn't remember being ordered—I could always ask to confirm it with the doctor in charge.

This was also a time when Paul and I constantly modified Jillian's environment to serve her within the context of her disabilities. As she grew, we found furniture, equipment, and toys that either helped her access life, or helped us to care for her. We got an adaptive shower chair so I could bathe her while standing next to her outside the shower. We bought two huge beanbag chairs for use in different rooms, and a padded therapy table we set up in our family room. She loved music, so we bought her CDs and musical toys. I also purchased age-appropriate items, like a Barbie doll that came in a wheelchair, hair accessories, nail polish, scented lotions, and lighted room decorations. My favorite was a beaded curtain that hung in her doorway. Every time we pushed her into her room, she passed through it, causing a cascade of sound.

We already lived in a ranch home built in the 50s, so it was mostly wheelchair-accessible. The open floor plan and large rooms made it easy to use her wheelchair and other equipment. But the family room was sunken, so we renovated the house to be on one level, at the same time adding a screened-in porch and a patio. It served her and us well, as we could then have her with us in any room in the house. Living in Nashville, the outdoor screened porch was usable for much of the year, and Jillian spent many hours there, hearing birdsong, watching Rachel play in her Winnie-the-Pooh playhouse, or listening to everyone chatting at dinner.

One of the best local places to take Jillian was our neighborhood pool, just a few miles away. Sequoia Swim Club has an airy, covered dining pavilion, and trees surround the pool deck and playground. We spent many summers there, where Jillian could rest in the shade while I swam with Rachel and the boys. I even took Jillian into the water for some of the time. When the pool was warm enough, it was her favorite place on earth! She enjoyed the buoyancy and ease of movement. She loved the other kids splashing and playing around her. Even as she grew bigger and heavier, in the pool I could hold her in my arms for a long time. On those days, I often brought a picnic dinner so Paul could join us after work. We usually stayed until the pool closed at dark. Those were happy times, wheelchair and all. Later, when Rachel was a preschooler and needed me to take her to the bathroom, the boys would hold Jillian in their arms in the pool. This always prompted remarks from others at the pool about how kindly the boys treated Jillian. In fact, when they took care of Rachel for me while I was with Jillian, other moms commented on how good they were with Rachel. I always felt this was because they knew what they had lost in Jillian, and they never took Rachel for granted.

Whether at home, at the pool, or on a trip, Paul and I developed a good partnership in Jillian's care. I assumed the role of primary caregiver, as he was working all day. He participated in major medical appointments and always served as my sounding board for decisions or challenges. Since he spent his days tending to sick children, it was important for him to be Jillian's daddy first of all. We agreed on a system where I saved up medical questions for a certain time when we could walk together and discuss them. This helped me break my habit of constantly badgering him with any medical thought that came through my mind. Paul often felt the burden of not being able to cure Jillian, but it did make him a better doctor. Today he sees several Rett patients and has his share of patients with special needs. The lessons he learned caring for Jillian have made him more humble, wise, and empathetic. Jillian loved for Paul to carry her and twirl her around. For years, he acted out stories at bedtime using the row of stuffed animals on her bed. And he pushed her on many walks—like up the steep path to Native American ruins in Arizona. I am not sure a wheelchair had been up there before! We sometimes grieved separately along the way, as Jillian's life and struggles affected us individually, but we both fought hard to create a positive family experience.

With Jillian's transition to kindergarten, Paul and I wondered how best to educate her in this phase of her life. I began investigating available options, and together we tried to hear where God was directing us to place Jillian. I visited our local public elementary school's "Life Skills" classroom, which was a special-education classroom in a regular school. Students in this program were mainstreamed as much as they were able. Unfortunately, for Jillian this would have meant only classes such as music and lunch. Also, this classroom had as many as ten students who were all at different ages, diagnoses, and levels of functioning or cognition. One teacher and an assistant staffed it.

Like when I researched preschools, I was nervous for Jillian. She was easy to ignore and could not advocate for herself in this kind of setting. I also visited a local private Montessori school and spoke with the head of admissions. They did not hesitate to welcome Jillian, and they had a vision for her inclusion in the peaceful and warm classroom. This school's willingness to partner with us on our journey amazed me. They did not know my family but were obviously already committed to the idea that people with special needs have value and can be included. Because we would have had to pay both for tuition and for an assistant, we decided not to pursue this path, but it was a gift to me that they welcomed her. We were not certain how cognitively impaired Jillian was, so we wanted to teach her things typical kids learn in kindergarten and first grade.

Since kindergarten our boys had attended Christ Presbyterian Academy, a K-12 private Christian school in Nashville. The administrators and staff had been supportive of us since Jillian's diagnosis. Now that she was of school age, I wanted advice from the principal, Anne Purdy. After I had described all the schools I had visited and the various options, Mrs. Purdy paused, then looked me in the eye and said, "Don't you think it would mean so much to the boys to have their sister in their school?" I had not really considered this option, as CPA is not set up to teach special education. But as we continued to talk, we came up with a plan where Jillian could attend CPA two mornings a week with an assistant we would provide, and I would homeschool her the other days.

Thus began several years of homeschooling. Each day until lunch, I had help with Jillian. The assistants followed a loose curriculum with weekly and monthly topics around which we centered activities. They also did therapy with her as part of her school morning, and danced in our living room or took her outside as weather allowed. We used adaptive learning tools and toys as well as standard books and manipulatives. She learned about animals, seasons, occupations, and basic things like letters and numbers. All this was simply presented to her, as she could not respond or give any indication that she understood. She did "attend" (the special education word for "pay attention") most of the time, so we felt that something was going on. And she was happy. Her team of caregivers enjoyed her and worked hard to be creative. By the end of the year, I had a box full of papers and projects she had participated in with eye contact or "hand-over-hand"—the term for a teacher putting their hand over the student's hand and guiding the action.

Jillian also loved her two mornings at CPA, and the children accepted her completely. She attended Cindy Anderson's classroom, where she came alive in their morning circle times. Once during their morning worship, when Jillian was responding to the music and her peers' singing, one of her classmates said to her teacher, "Mrs. Anderson, I see the glory of God all over her!" Many of the students in her class that year were in hard places. One student's father had died of a heart attack while he was playing with her. Another was in the process of losing his brother to leg cancer. Having Jillian in their midst, sitting peacefully in her wheelchair in all her brokenness, allowed students to be vulnerable with their own weaknesses or suffering. When the class went to P.E. or outside to recess, students clamored over who could push the wheelchair. Jillian's assistant, Jane Carroll, had to keep a list in her pocket of which student was next in line to push Jillian in order to keep the peace! This class was in fifth grade when Jillian died, and Anne Purdy spoke to the entire grade about her life and death. Here is a letter her teacher, Cindy, wrote to us after Jillian died:

> I think of your family and Jillian so often. My heart has been sad, and yet very grateful to have known Jillian. What a gift from God she has been to so many. The precious times that I was with her, I learned so much, and she never said a word. I learned that there is truly power in the powerless, and that it is in being who God created us to be that we reflect His love. And I saw children respond as they saw "the glory of God all over her"...When I think of Jillian dancing in the presence of her Abba Father, my heart smiles.

I watched those students from her Kindergarten class grow up and graduate, and it never made me sad to see them. I could rejoice in their successes because they had been her friends. In addition to her times at school, Jillian made friends at church. She attended her regular Sunday School class and, as part of our house church, got to know many other families. Out of those families came many local surrogate aunts, uncles, and cousins.

Our extended biological family—none closer than an eight-hour drive—responded well to Jillian's disabilities and supported us as best they could. Families react differently to children with special needs. Some feel awkward or feel the child cannot participate in regular activities, so they accidentally or intentionally communicate rejection. We were fortunate that our families welcomed us with Jillian. I cannot imagine our journey without them. Even though they were far away, they never judged, avoided, or condemned us. They received Jillian in their homes, pushed through any initial discomfort they might have had, and treated her like any other child. We participated in many fun family reunions in California, Sanibel Island in Florida, and at my mother and father's country home in Pennsylvania. My widowed mother-in-law lived by herself, remained in good health, and visited frequently, helping to take care of whatever child needed taking care of, including Jillian. She spent many hours reading to Jillian and, later, walking up and down our driveway and street pushing her while the other kids played in the yard. On our trip to the Grand Canyon, we visited Paul's sister and her husband in Arizona. When we pushed Jillian up that narrow paved trail to a Pueblo cliff dwelling, Paul's sister and husband did not laugh at us but supported us in our desire to be a family together. Our other siblings came around us in a similar way.

When Jillian was nine, my father received a sudden diagnosis of melanoma skin cancer. He was told he had three months left, and indeed that is how long he lived. My siblings and I took turns helping with his treatment and care near Pittsburgh. I was there in the early summer with all four of my kids. Their youthful presence lightened the more somber mood in my parents' home. The boys took care of Rachel for me, but I kept

Jillian in her chair or sitting in her big beanbag chair. As I would wheel my father past Jillian, he would stop and speak to her. Or if she was fussy, he would stop and empathize with her pain: "Poor child…sweet little girl…" He connected with her then in a way he never had before. Her bravery touched him when he himself needed courage. My mother, herself disabled from fifty years of rheumatoid arthritis, often sat in her own wheelchair in our midst. She has taught us much about the redemption of suffering in walking out her own journey of pain and joy. Over the years, I often parked Jillian's chair next to my mother's wheelchair, and they enjoyed one another's companionship.

When I look back through photo albums of our family life, I see Jillian in her chair, parked by Christmas stockings being opened, tables filled with holiday food, candles being blown out on cakes, or children playing games in our yard. When she was with us, I remember being frustrated that I could never get a good still picture of her because she could not smile or even make eye contact on command. Her pictures rarely made me happy, as they seemed to capture her brokenness more than her life. But now as I look at those same pictures, I see her watching us or see a brother holding her hand or see her listening to a book being read. Our life was full and rich, and Jillian was a major player in that story.

Jillian in kindergarten, at a Cub Scout jamboree with Luke and Joyce, and on a trail at the headwaters of the Colorado River with Paul.

Jillian as a preschooler with the boys, then as an elementary student. Rachel is now in the pictures!

Chapter 4

Running from Suffering

I can speak with some assurance only of how God was present in that dark time for me in the sense that I was not destroyed by it but came out of it with scars that I bear to this day, to be sure, but also somehow the wiser and the stronger for it...I think that I learned something about how even tragedy can be a means of grace that I might never have come to any other way.

Frederick Beuchner

I want to pause here to address the problem of suffering. This time in Jillian's life, when she was in a place of relative peace, allowed me to read and find purpose for her suffering and mine. Ultimately, I decided that Jillian's pain and mine had purpose and that our lives and those around us would be positively changed, not just in spite of suffering but because of it. First I would like to address the moral questions of: Would my life have been better without Jillian? Would I have aborted her if I had known? Would it have been better for her not to exist than to have suffered so much? Then I would like to guide you down the path I stumbled along on my way to embracing suffering as a terrible gift. Next, I will explore the mystery of touching human brokenness and its profound impact on us. Finally, I would like to consider miraculous healing.

To Suffer or Not To Suffer: The Moral Dilemma

Toward the end of Jillian's life, scientists discovered the Rett gene—the specific genetic deletion that causes the constellation of Rett symptoms. This brought prenatal screening for Rett closer to reality. The incidence of terminating babies thought to have Down syndrome has risen dramatically over the past decades. As I considered what a mother would do, confronted with the knowledge that she would have a daughter with Rett, I grieved. Choosing to proceed on a path that would be painful for you and your child, possibly damaging your marriage and your other children, brings a moral dilemma.

Our society strives to eliminate pain or at best preemptively strike when pain is on the horizon. In the United States, we are insulated from warzone death, chronic illness, abject poverty, and starving hunger. We are not like most of the world, where countless families have lost mothers, fathers, brothers, and sisters to AIDs or terrorism or famine. We are afraid to suffer, and avoiding suffering has become a moral obligation if not a moral right.

What if we are wrong? What if humans grow through suffering and overcoming, and we have removed that dimension from human experience? Our desire to get rid of germs in the environment has led to a new generation of children with weak immune systems. Have we similarly weakened our ability to allow tragedy to transform us?

An interaction with two different moms shed light on these thoughts. When I was pregnant with our first child, I worked at local hospitals with a support group for parents experiencing a high-risk pregnancy or birth. I interviewed moms who had been on bed rest or had newborns in the intensive care unit for a monthly newsletter. I also had an opportunity to hear several women who had abortions for medical reasons talk about their experiences in a clinical, non-religious setting. One mom I interviewed and one mom at the post-abortion seminar had each been pregnant with babies who had anencephaly. I learned so much about the value of choosing pain from hearing their parallel, yet radically different stories.

Anencephaly is a condition where the neural tube—the immature spinal cord and brain—does not form properly at the top end of the tube, where the brain is. The most common neural tube defect is spina bifida, where the neural tube is poorly formed or unsealed, exposing the spinal cord at the base of the back. When the defect is in the brain area, the condition is universally fatal. The babies remain alive in utero, but upon birth they either have brain and spinal cord defects that are incompatible with life, or their brains are well-formed but are exposed to the air and quickly become infected once they are born.

The mother I interviewed for the newsletter had been pregnant with twins. Ultrasound showed that one of the twins had anencephaly. Abortion of the affected twin could have endangered the healthy twin, so the mother carried both to term. I will never forget her sharing how her husband was present in the delivery room and how horrified he was at the appearance of the affected twin. Babies with this condition usually die just hours after birth. But this child did not die. The healthy twin arrived safely, and both babies went home with mom and dad from the hospital. The affected twin lived three weeks. Mom had pictures of the two boys together, and with his little cap on, the affected twin was gorgeous. Dad spent time holding him. Mom even tried to nurse him, and he opened his eyes and looked at her, two things he was not supposed to be able to do. As I listened to this mom, her grief mingled with her gratitude. She knew her son and had held him and loved him for three precious weeks. The boys slept together as infants. The healthy twin, growing up, would see pictures of his brother.

The other mother, who told her story at the post-abortion seminar, described how her child's diagnosis of anencephaly also appeared on ultrasound. So this mom chose an abortion, which was followed by a procedure to clean out the uterus called a D and C (dilation and curettage). The child had no chance of survival; if born, it would have to die, perhaps uncomfortably, and the pregnancy itself had its own risks. The decision made sense. Yet as I heard her describe the cold metal plates under her feet and the hard table, the sterile surroundings, the departure from the office like she'd only had her teeth cleaned, I heard so much grief. Stark, empty, unresolved grief.

Humans throughout history have avoided suffering when possible. Like the need to eat, the instinct to survive propels us away from pain. Today, when we read of cultures in the past sacrificing their children to ensure a good harvest or to bring rain, we judge them as barbaric, even selfish. How could you throw away the life of your sixteen-year-old daughter for some legend or curse? Ancient peoples were not intrinsically more evil or heartless than we are. They simply believed that their lives and perhaps the lives of their whole village would go better if they sacrificed their children. Abortion can be a similar deception. If I kill this child, my life and perhaps the lives of my family members will be better.

What inalienable right do I have to a perfect life? I am not trying to address whether we should or should not have abortions; I am asking, why do we do it? What about an elderly person no longer useful to society? Who is to say their life has no impact on those around them? Should they be euthanized so I don't have to suffer taking care of them? Do I have a right to leave a marriage because it is not all I had hoped for and it causes me pain? I know pain has ruined many lives, and I am not proposing simple solutions. I merely want to ask if pain can actually bring me, my family, and my community strength and joy, when lived with Jesus and redeemed through Him. The possibility that pain could be transformed, that what was intended for evil could be turned to good, fueled my life with Jillian.

A couple in our church has two sons. Both boys have Duchene's muscular dystrophy, and I have watched them grow up. They have gone from running toddlers to halting elementary students to wheelchair-bound adolescents to dependent adults. From outward appearances, four tragic lives. But those boys have inspired their parents, and that family inspires all who meet them. The mother told me an amazing story about her youngest, then in high school. Every lunchtime at his public school, Daniel sat with his group of friends, and one of them helped lift Daniel's arm holding the utensil with his food on it, to his mouth. I love that picture: Daniel's suffering calling out the best in those around him. This holy event will affect those young friends for their lifetime. We fear suffering as an empty place, but it is full of God's presence.

Yet we run away from suffering and embrace the humaneness of not allowing children to suffer. I do not know whether it would have been better for me or for Jillian if she had never been born. But after living through grief and seeing the positive impact that pressing through suffering to joy had on my family, including Jillian and me, I cannot advocate avoidance.

A Path Through the Wilderness: Suffering Has a Purpose

Viktor E. Frankl wrote *Man's Search for Meaning* about his experiences as a prisoner in World War II:

> We who lived in concentration camps can remember the men who walked through the huts comforting others, giving away their last piece of bread. They may have been few in number, but they offer sufficient proof that everything can be taken from a man but one thing: the last of the human freedoms—to choose one's attitude in

> any given set of circumstances, to chose one's own way...The way in which a man accepts his fate and all the suffering it entails, the way in which he takes up his cross, gives him ample opportunity—even under the most difficult circumstances—to add a deeper meaning to his life.[1]

Coming from a Protestant Presbyterian and then charismatic background, I firmly believed God was sovereign and also could do miracles. But with Jillian, I confronted a circumstance that demanded daily understanding in order to proceed. Was this something I just had to get through stoically? Was this something I could pray away or change with my faith level? Neither of these paths seemed productive. I did not have a frame of reference in which to process my suffering. This section contains answers I discovered on my journey through the land of suffering—both my own suffering and the suffering of my child. Henri Nouwen writes:

> Who can save a child from a burning house without taking the risk of being hurt by the flames?...In short, 'Who can take away suffering without entering it?' The greatest illusion of leadership is to think that others can be led out of the desert by someone who has never been there.[2]

Isaiah 53:3 describes Jesus as "a man of sorrows, and acquainted with grief." I, too, am now acquainted with grief. I have been in and through the desert. These stories and reflections map my way out.

Desperately trying to find some words that could help me process my anguish, fear, and questions, I went to our local Christian bookstore. I was not looking for books that talk about why bad things happen in life or how to get out of my situation. I wanted to hear from people who had experienced tragedy and walked through it with God. I stumbled upon some devotionals highlighting the writings of earlier Christians such as Francis of Assisi and Augustine of Hippo. Augustine says, "And so it is in coming to you daily—weak, hungry and in need of your Life flowing through me—that my troubled and darkened soul gradually gains in strength."[3]

Francis writes:

> Among men, we may search for someone who can understand our heaviest griefs, but will find no one. We may long for a friend who can be always present, giving words that console and comfort, but we will look in vain (Psalm 69:18-20). He alone is our sweet holy Father! He is also king, God of the whole creation. And He stoops to listen…comes to our help (Psalm 44:4-8).[4]

Then I began reading excerpts from John of the Cross, a friar, mystic, and religious reformer who lived in 16th century Spain. I read how it was in the "dark night of his soul" that he encountered God in a deeper, more intimate way than he ever had. For his beliefs, he was imprisoned in a cell so small he could not lie down. At first, he felt abandoned by God. But in that cell he encountered the "living flame of God" and experienced divine love so powerfully that he spent the rest of his life writing about it. Some time later, he discovered that his cell was unlocked and escaped into the night. But it was *before* his deliverance that he encountered God.

John of the Cross described human experience from birth through adulthood as largely based on the things we perceive through our senses. Even after we become Christian's we use our senses to establish our reality and can ignore spiritual perception, which is interior and directed by the Holy Spirit. John urges, "As long as we see only with our bodily eyes, we will continue to live like a blind captive, fumbling around inside a prison cell in the dark of night—while all the time the door that leads to our freedom stands open." John proposed a way to negotiate out of darkness into the light and love of God: "Trust Him to lead you out of darkness, fear, misunderstanding, and doubt…Then you will find the thing your heart longs for—perfect peace and freedom in the presence of the Lord, who is the Lover of your soul."[5] Applied to my situation, I had the real crisis of parenting a child with multiple, severe disabilities. Jillian had the assignment of living in a body that did not respond to her commands or desires. We both had our prisons—how could the door be open, how could the Spirit guide us to make our escape? Could we both find the connection with God and joy in living? As I continued to read John of the Cross, I felt that I too could experience the love of God in the middle of my suffering with Jillian. And Jillian herself did not have just to endure, but she could be transformed through her sorrow.

At the same time, I realized that the cost was high. Ongoing life with Jillian was hard. It required continual denial of self, continual grieving for her, continual struggling for our family to have a great life together. Any day that I got up and felt like I had strength for the day inevitably ended badly. Jillian would have a big seizure, or throw up all her food, or need her whole bed changed from faulty diapers. Finally I took a white cloth diaper and tied it to a stick, like a flag. I put it in my bedroom so every morning when I woke up I would see it and remember to surrender right away! If God did not carry me and our family, we were crushed. There is no middle ground in suffering. It either destroys you, or you are forced to be better than you were before. Another saint of old, Julian of Norwich, said, "If there is anywhere on earth a lover of God who is always kept safe, I know nothing of it, for it was not shown to me. But this was shown: that in falling and rising again we are always kept in that same precious love."

This is a letter I wrote to my mom during this time of searching and reading. I include it because it is one of the few things I actually wrote when Jillian was young. So it expresses how I felt at the time, not just in retrospect. My mother has had rheumatoid arthritis for over fifty years. When I wrote her this letter, she had been through multiple joint replacement surgeries, years of chronic pain, and increasing disability.

> I've been reading John of the Cross as well as a devotional by Amy Carmichael. Are you familiar with her? She was from Northern Ireland I believe and went to India in 1895 as a missionary to orphans and to rescue girls from temple prostitution. Anyway, she was stricken with illness that left her confined to her bed for about 20 years. She ran the mission from her bed and spent most of her time in prayer and writing down the things she had gleaned from the Bible. I was especially struck this week by her words concerning being "lifted up" by God. She had many verses like James 4:10: "Be made low in

the presence of the Lord and He will lift you up," and Psalm 147:6: "The Lord lifteth up the meek." The sentence that caught my spirit was, "As I pondered this word from the Psalm and thought of the Lord's life, always triumphant, never cast down by disappointment, by weariness, by apparent failure, or even the certainty of suffering swiftly drawing nearer, I wondered if the cause of our cast-down hours is not the hardness of the way (as we are tempted to think it is), but some flaw in the inner spirit which makes it impossible for our God to lift us up. If so, praise Him, it need not remain so: There is a lifting up."

This hit me because I remember being up with Jillian night after night and being joyful as I allowed God to carry me, but then something would happen that would so discourage me or anger me that I would almost say to God, "All right, this is it. I draw the line here!" Which was indeed like shooting myself in the foot because it did not change the circumstances and it prevented me from allowing the Lord to lift me up! And it was only when I broke that place in my rebellious soul that I could receive His help (or my husband's for that matter!).

John of the Cross would understand this too, since his thrust is: get your eyes off your circumstances and on Jesus. I reread the intro and the first devotional selection yesterday. I was reminded again how we must fight with our spirit to pull our mind, will, and emotions into submission. I love the image John uses of being in a cell, fumbling around, while all the while the door that leads to freedom stands open. There seems to be such power in just saying, "I know what I am experiencing is not the whole reality. God will lift me up. He will lead me out of this cell. Maybe not the way I want him to, but in the best way."

You and I have been through big storms these past few years. Now we are in a lull. While we enjoy this season of peace, we must not put our hope in it. We must learn what we can, for storms are in our future, and God has a glorious plan for that time as well as this. Like Paul, we must learn the secret of being content in all situations. I also love the phrase "Lover of my soul" because it seems that in order to trust God we must believe that he loves us. A friend was talking with me about authority and that in order to have true authority you must have love. That applies to human relationships certainly. A child who feels tangibly the love of their parents will receive their authority. A wife who discerns love from her husband will submit. If she submits without love there is bitterness. How much more with God! It is only as we experience His love that we can receive His control over our lives. Lamentations says that nothing comes but through the hand of God. Wow! That means that he lets bad things happen but out of love. I so want to grow in His love so that I can receive what he has for me out of every circumstance.

At the beginning of our journey, Paul and I drew inspiration from Christopher de Vinck's book *The Power of the Powerless*, about his severely handicapped brother Oliver. Oliver de Vinck was born April 20, 1947, six months after his mother lost consciousness due to gas leaking from the family's stove. While Catherine de Vinck lay without oxygen for several minutes,

Oliver in her womb also was deprived of oxygen. Shortly after birth, Catherine realized that Oliver was blind and mute, and had suffered extensive brain injury. Oliver's parents refused to institutionalize him and instead took one doctor's advice to "take him home and love him." Later, Christopher wrote an essay about his brother for the *Wall Street Journal*, and it immediately impacted the nation. Christopher explains the effect living with Oliver had on him:

> Oliver still remains the most hopeless human being I ever met, the weakest human being I ever met, and yet he was one of the most powerful human beings I ever met. As a teacher, I spend many hours preparing my lessons, hoping that I can influence my students in small, significant ways. Thousands of books are printed each year with the hope that the authors can move people to action. We all labor at the task of raising our children, teaching them values, hoping something "gets through" to them after all our efforts. Oliver could do absolutely nothing except breathe, sleep, eat, and yet he was responsible for action, love, courage, insight.[6]

Later, he compiled that original essay with letters he had received from around the nation and a section written by his mother. Her description of her emotions surrounding the tragic news of Oliver's diagnosis expressed what I had felt so keenly. She writes:

> It's hard to express what such a verdict means to a mother. It pierced me to my depth, ripped apart the very fabric of life when we discovered how severely different

> Oliver was going to be all his life. It was not something one could put aside or escape. The world appeared darkened: it was as if the whole of reality had been covered with a gray film. I didn't understand yet.[7]

She goes on to describe how she began to understand the gift Oliver was to her and her other children. By the time Oliver was older and she attended a special benediction for the sick in Europe, she realized her deepest prayer for Oliver had shifted. "My whole being was aching to ask that Oliver be healed, for I knew that Jesus of Nazareth was passing by, and my child and I were in need. But I stood there, transfixed, able to pray only for purity of heart."[8]

She concludes with how taking care of Oliver transformed her:

> Looking at him, I saw the power of powerlessness. His total helplessness speaks to our deepest hearts, calls us not merely to pious emotions but to service. Through this child, I felt bound to Christ crucified—yes, and also to all those who suffer in the world.[9]

Hearing from a mother at different points in her journey meant so much to me. Similarly, one of Paul's favorite parts from Christopher's original essay is a quote from his father:

> I asked my father, "How did you care for Oliver for thirty-two years?"
> "It was not thirty-two years," he said. "I just asked myself, 'Can I feed Oliver today?' and the answer was always, 'Yes I can.'"[10]

Many times I have returned to this idea that we can bear what God has for us today, one day at a time. We do not need to carry the days to come.

The temptation to simply survive—to just get through it and pick up the pieces on the other side—is great. But an encounter with the story of famous Antarctic explorer Ernest Shackleton showed me how dangerous it is to just survive. His story is one of the greatest survival stories on record. After having his ship run aground and frozen into the ice shelf for the winter, he kept all his crew alive. Later, he set out over the snow and braved the ocean in a small boat to get help from a remote island. Against all odds, he made it to the island, and when the rescuers returned, they were able to save the crew.

PBS ran a special on his journey and rescue. I had my boys watch it because it was so inspirational—or so I assumed. But what became apparent on the show, through interviews with surviving crewmembers and their families, was how ruined their lives were afterwards. You would think surviving something like that would give you fuel for the days to come. After all, they had overcome and been saved. But they were all broken men, especially Shackleton. Apparently, just surviving was not enough. In fact, Shackleton had been so driven to survive, he had been quite abusive to his crew. They had survived, but the cost was great. On a subsequent voyage to Antarctica, he returned to his docked ship in a drunken stupor, had a heart attack, and died alone.

I did not want to just survive. I did not want to get to the end of the journey with Jillian and find my husband, my marriage, and my other children ruined in my attempt to make it. Surely if God had called us to this difficult thing, His mercy and power would be there to get us through it unharmed. Surely my boys could be better men because of Jillian. Surely Paul and I could have a vibrant relationship as we partnered to take care of our family, and not just hope to avoid divorce. Mere survival was not the path I wanted.

A common myth in Christianity is that God has promised to remove hardship from us if we follow him. If your life has problems, it is easy to feel that it is your fault. You have made bad choices or have little faith or have missed God. A gentleman came to our church during this time and gave the Sunday message. He spoke about the parable of the man who built his house upon the rock. He pointed out that Jesus says, "The man who hears my words and puts them into practice is like the man who builds his house upon a rock…When the storms come…" Here he paused and said that storms *will* come. That is a given. Both men in the story experience storms. The difference is how they are prepared for those storms. The house on the rock stood, but the house on sand "fell with a great crash" (Matthew 7:27). Storms, suffering, and death are part of the broken world we live in. As Christians, we are not exempt from the fallen system of this world, but we do have different tools to handle the storms and, ultimately, achieve a different outcome.

For as long as I can remember, I have been drawn to God. But it was in my fifth-grade Sunday School class that I heard that God still works in our lives today. I read a comic-book version of Corrie ten Boom's *The Hiding Place.* Corrie and her family hid Jews in their home in Holland during World War II, helping many escape to freedom before Nazi soldiers discovered their hiding place and arrested the family. The hopeful story of Corrie's deliverance, how much God took care of her in the prison camp, and also her life once she got out, showed me that God still works today in the lives of His children. I could not deny that God had miraculously released her from a German concentration camp. Over the years, I have read nearly all her books.

Now with Jillian I remembered that Corrie's sister, Betsy, had died in the concentration camp. Betsy was perhaps closer to God—she certainly encouraged Corrie constantly. Corrie's father had also hidden Jews and died for it. So many had died! Dietrich Bonhoeffer, a prominent German Christian who resisted Hitler, was hanged days before Allied troops liberated his prison. I began to see that, while Corrie's deliverance was still miraculous, Betsy's perseverance and Bonhoeffer's peace were just as miraculous. God could intervene on your behalf and you still might not be rescued. You could suffer and die and still receive His provision. There were no guarantees of outcome—only guarantees of His provision in the trial.

Survival was not the goal, and neither was miraculous rescue, so what was the point? I began to think that it mattered how we lived out our situation with Jesus, and in fact our "living out" was the theatre of God's provision and transforming work. A practical example of this came to our family one day in 2002. My son Andrew is a faithful Tennessee Titans football fan. At age 11, he idolized quarterback Steve McNair and many other players on the team. One day we were watching a game that the Titans clearly could not win. Even though the last quarter still remained, the injuries the Titans had, the way they were playing, and the strength of the other team made victory impossible. Andrew shut off the TV in disgust. He angrily derided our team.

"Wait," I said. "Sometimes you have to play, even if you know you're going to lose. Steve McNair has to get out there and lead his team and play well, even though it is hopeless. Tell me a battle in our lives we know we are going to lose unless God intervenes miraculously."

"Jillian," he responded.

"Yes," I said, "and how we play the game out matters. Any team can look good when they are winning, but we want our team to be good when they are losing."

We turned the TV back on and supported our team the rest of the game until they lost.

Playing out a losing game or living well through painful circumstances meant embracing suffering as an inescapable life-variable. How we lived it mattered. Perhaps suffering could be viewed as a terrible gift, which, like harsh lighting, brought clear perspective to things that were important and true and real. Jesus embraced suffering and sought out those who were broken. In ministering to the broken and in being broken ourselves, we experience solidarity with Jesus and find ourselves on holy ground.

Taking Care of the Least of These

It is hard for parents to see any child suffer. But to see the suffering of a handicapped child creates an even greater pain.[9]

Henri Nouwen

It is hard at times to see and hear the event which is right in front of you, the event of true love.[10]

Henri Nouwen

The most influential literary companion on my journey into suffering was Henri Nouwen. Nouwen was a professor, priest, and writer. By his late middle age, he was a well-known Harvard professor. But Nouwen, dissatisfied with his great literary success, his popularity, and even his mission trips to South America, felt there was something more.

His friend Jean Vanier, who had started communities for handicapped people, invited Henri to join him at L'Arche ("The Ark"), a community of homes in France. There Nouwen heard Jean Vanier characterize the call to work long-term with handicapped people as becoming poor: "I was deeply struck with Jean's remark: 'Jesus did not say, "Happy are those who serve the poor," but "Happy are the poor."' Being poor is what Jesus invites us to, and that is much, much harder than serving the poor."[11] Jean Vanier believed that people with special needs have much to share with those around them, and he pioneered living environments where caregivers could live in partnership with disabled community members.

Unlike a typical group home, the idea is that all members contribute to the community, and everyone needs the other equally. But living there requires a fundamental shift in what we perceive as valuable or important. Nouwen describes his experience of living in this community in France, receiving what each individual brings:

> It is a humble life in which joy is hidden in small corners, always there to be found but never separate from much pain. The rewards are small but very real: Philippe smiles, Jean-Luc looks you in the eye, Gerard gives a hug, Michelle sleeps a whole night, Sylvienne says one more word.[12]

As recorded in Nouwen's book *The Road to Daybreak*, he spent nine months at L'Arche in France. He also spent several weeks at Daybreak, the L'Arche community in Canada. At Daybreak, Nouwen went to a meeting of assistants and heard from Nick, the head of the woodworking shop, how hard it was to balance making a good product and facilitating a meaningful experience for the handicapped individuals who worked with him:

> It asks for a deep inner conviction that a slow job done together is better than a fast job done alone…I found this out myself this afternoon when I went apple picking with Janice, Carol, Adam, Rose, and their assistants. My attitude was to get the apples picked, put them in bags, and go home. But I soon learned that all of that was much less important than to help Rose pick one or two apples, to walk with Janice looking for apples that hang low enough so that she herself can reach them, to compliment Carol on her ability to find good apples, and just to sit beside Adam in his wheelchair under an apple tree and give him a sense of belonging to the group.[13]

The community and its individual members deeply impacted Nouwen, and he felt closer to God than ever before. He had been on a climb to success but had missed the call of Jesus, which is not upward. He says, "I began to feel the tension between these two ways very strongly. And I decided to choose something else. I chose to follow my calling, the way down that leads to the poor, the weak and the sorrowful."[14] *The Road to Daybreak* records Nouwen's transition from academia to his belief that he was called to minister as a priest for Daybreak.

Before he left France, Nouwen gave a teaching about the word "glory" in the Gospel of John. This teaching contrasts God's glory with human glory: "Human glory is the result of being considered better, faster, more beautiful, more powerful, or more successful than others. Glory conferred by people is glory which results from being favorably compared to other people." He goes on to describe how human glory relies on upward mobility, gaining more with each success, and how it leads to darkness: "Human glory, based on competition, leads to rivalry; rivalry carries within it the beginning of violence; and violence is the way to death." He then describes God's glory as illustrated in John's Gospel. He points out that Jesus did not come to be the best in a competitive way, but to suffer with us: "God chose the way of downward mobility. Every time Jesus speaks about being glorified and giving glory, he always refers to his humiliation and death." Only after Jesus experienced the highest level of humiliation and suffering on the cross did he experience the glory of resurrection. Nouwen finishes, "The risen Lord always shows us his wounds. This is the deepest reason for living in solidarity with poor, oppressed, and handicapped people. They are the ones through whom God's glory can manifest itself to us."[15]

Nouwen gave up his prestigious faculty position and moved to Toronto. He spent the rest of his life serving there as a priest and writing. In addition, he lived in a home and took care of a man with disabilities named Adam. This caregiving intimacy with Adam taught Henri much about Jesus and himself. His book *Adam, God's Beloved*, as well as others written during this time, reflects his growth while in this community. Here Nouwen speaks about Adam in a movie made about Nouwen shortly before Nouwen's death:

> In this house Adam is the central person. Adam in his weakness creates this community. In his dependence he's asking the supporters to love one another. What he's really saying is, "I'm living out of your mutual love. Your love is necessary for me to live well." When we don't like each other the quality of his life gets worse. So he's like the tie of this community. In a way he's my professor.

Nouwen learned many things from taking care of Adam that resonated with my experiences with Jillian. They articulated and expanded on things I had observed in the way Jillian brought our family together. They asked me to be present to her as a person, not a project. Nouwen continues about Adam in the movie:

> I've also learned that he is as complete as I am. He's not just partly human. He's a complete human being. He has a heart that can love and wants to be loved. It doesn't matter if one can talk. It is important to have a heart, so one can love and receive love.

I also began to see how brokenness and weakness—which we all despise in ourselves—was just as precious to God as success and accomplishment. Even those with a natural gifting toward mercy and compassion can extend easily for the weak in their community, but often do not extend that grace to themselves. Nouwen shares how he learned this with Adam:

> He reveals God to us in his weakness. Blessed are the poor in spirit. I think Jesus meant: Blessed are we in our

> weak areas. My poverty differs from Adam's poverty. It's not so much that I'm rich and he's poor. He's just more dependent, more crippled. In his lameness and poverty he is a blessed person. Through him I've discovered my own poverty. My impatience…my lusts…my desire to be successful. My violence. I have to believe that God is present in these things. I've learned more about my poverty…and I've learned that I'm blessed in these areas. It's significant Jesus didn't say: Blessed is he who takes care of the poor. No, blessed are the poor. Not: blessed is he who brings comfort. Blessed are the sorrowful. So blessing is found in spiritual poverty.[16]

A blessing rests on those who are broken, and simply allowing them to be present with us mysteriously changes us. Not only those with special needs, but also the elderly, or those who are very ill and not lucid, have purpose, dignity, and relevance. In summarizing his experiences in his book *In the Name of Jesus*, Nouwen writes,

> These broken, wounded, and completely unpretentious people forced me to let go of my relevant self—the self that can do things, show things, prove things, build things—and forced me to reclaim that unadorned self in which I am completely vulnerable, open to receive and give love regardless of any accomplishments.[17]

Nouwen's work impacted me deeply as he discovered the mysteries of human brokenness, both the obvious and the hidden. I started reading anything I could by him, especially writings from his L'Arche season. On top of all I had read from the saints of old, Nouwen gave me vision for this life of suffering—both Jillian's and mine. He articulated the effect I had felt of Jillian's brokenness on my life and the lives of others. He gave me hope that this was a sacred journey.

WHAT ABOUT HEALING?

Part of what it means to believe in God, at least part of what it means for me, is to believe in the possibility of miracles.[18]

Frederick Beuchner

Inner conflict about miraculous healing arises from the expectation that God will surely show His love by removing pain and suffering. So the logical conclusion to remaining ill is that God does not care or that we are not worthy. Yet like a mathematical proof, we must start our "theorem" or logic with what we know—in this case, God is good—all subsequent conclusions cannot violate that starting truth. Theresa of Avila, friend of John of the Cross, said:

> There is only one thing in the whole world that we can offer you [Jesus], only one thing with which we "buy" the love of God, which you have promised to pour into our hearts by the Holy Spirit (Romans 5:5). The tribute you ask is that we love you deeply, and willingly give to you all—including the people we love, our belongings, our selves. Then we can begin to act on the trust we so

> boldly tell others about—really trusting that you are always and only a Good Lord![19]

Sometimes we have to accept truth that challenges our rational mind. I remember learning as a student that if A=B and B=C then A=C, otherwise known as the transitive property of equality. While I could understand this property, as a non-math student it did not take long for me to get in over my head in algebra. But just because I did not understand longer proofs based on this and other properties did not make them untrue. Similarly, "God is good" is one of the "truths" claimed in the Bible and must be treated as something to build on even when not fully understood.

In the midst of Jillian's first regression, I developed Raynaud's Syndrome. The joints of my feet and hands became extremely painful if they became a little cold and then warmed up. I purchased new shoes, socks, and gloves to try to keep this from happening. Still, it would sneak up on me and could be so disheartening with everything else going on. Paul is an elder at our church, and he had a meeting one night during this time. He asked for prayer for me. The elders prayed, and I was at home with the kids. I did not feel anything, or even know they were praying for me, but I never had another attack of Raynaud's. I consider that a miraculous healing. Had God healed me to show me in a tangible way that he was able to heal Jillian and therefore was *choosing* not to?

Since before we were married, Paul and I have attended a church that believes in the authority of the Bible, the importance of prayer, and the continued work of the Holy Spirit in modern times. People prayed for Jillian to be healed, but no one treated us as failures because she had not been healed. Jillian's illness was genetic. In other words, every cell in her body had the defect. This would be the same for a child with Down syndrome, cystic fibrosis, or muscular dystrophy. In contrast, diseases like cancer, muscular sclerosis, or arthritis attack the body but are outside the basic genetic cell structure. As we began to read more about healing, we could not discover a case of someone with a genetic error who had been healed.

Whenever I asked God about healing Jillian, I felt like he was standing close to me with love, but he was silent and sad. I still prayed for her healing, but I prayed more often for help to manage her situation and for her happiness and peace. Our son Andrew, two years Jillian's senior, prayed every night for years and years that she would be healed. I talked with him occasionally about this because I did not want him to get mad at God if his diligence did not pay off. At the same time, I did not want to tell him to stop. I always felt that God took all the prayers spoken for her healing from all our friends and family and applied them to other "accounts." She was a peaceful child with a happy life, and we had much joy during her season in our family. These were the fruits from all those prayers. She also brought life to people outside our family, which could be considered healing of a different nature. I came to the conclusion that what she and God were able to do together was more important than whether she could walk or talk.

As I studied the miracles in Scripture, I noticed they almost all had a purpose of greater significance than the individual act. This is most obvious in the gospel of John. When Jesus turned water into wine, John writes, "He thus revealed his glory, and his disciples put their faith in him" (John 2:11). Later, when the disciples ask Jesus whose fault it is that a man was born blind, Jesus answers, "Neither this man nor his parents sinned…But this happened so that the work of God might be displayed in his life" (John 9:3). This indicates that God wants to show up in our brokenness and be glorified. When Lazarus dies and Martha rebukes Jesus for not coming in time to save her brother, Jesus answers, "Did I not tell you that if you believed, you would see the glory of God?" (John 11:40). Even in the last chapter of John, Jesus indicates a miraculous deliverance is not always what will bring God glory. Jesus tells Peter that he, Peter, will have to walk out something he does not want to, and John says, "Jesus said this to indicate the kind of death by which Peter would glorify God" (John 21:19). The few examples of Jesus healing people in intimate and nonpublic moments still have greater meaning than the actual healing. He seems not to be saying, "I am sorry you are sick; let me take away this burden." Instead, he's saying, "So that you will know that I am God, let me remove this burden." Of course, scripture shows time and again that Jesus had great compassion on the suffering and wanted to make them whole, but healing was not the end point. Jesus used the gift of healing to draw a greater conclusion:

> Some men brought to [Jesus] a paralytic, lying on a mat…Jesus said, "Which is easier to say, 'Your sins are forgiven,' or to say, 'Get up and walk?' But so that you may know that the Son of Man has authority on earth to forgive sins…" Then he said to the paralytic, "Get up, take your mat and go home" (Matt. 9:5-6, NIV).

For the individual or the group, the miraculous always points to a greater knowledge of the glory of God.

A Contrast in Approaches

We had two experiences with famous faith healers. The first was with a man who has a great television presence and international fame. He came to Nashville for a healing conference at our big sports arena. I am not a fan of TV religious personalities of any kind, but I did not want my judgment or pride to keep me from receiving anything God had for us. The gospel of Luke shares a story where Jesus' disciples question the credentials of someone outside their group who is driving out demons. Jesus answers them, "Do not stop him, for whoever is not against you is for you" (Luke 9:50). Sometimes God uses vessels who do not meet our expectations to do His work. So we went one evening and unloaded Jillian with all the hundreds of others bringing broken bodies into the arena. As we stepped off the elevator from the garage, we were greeted by a female usher who said, "Are you ready for your miracle?" She did not really want our answer. It was more of an exhortation than a question.

Inside the arena, the stands were filled with people who could walk. All the wheelchairs were on the center floor. What a sea of hurting people and their caregivers! The family in front of us consisted of a young father, mother, and a girl with deformities who was about four. She was in her father's arms, writhing and crying. I watched all evening as her patient parents readjusted her, spoke soft words to her, and rocked her back and forth. The event started with advertisements, music, slideshows, and preaching. Hours went by, and the children were tired. Then handlers went into the audience and began pulling people out to go up on stage for prayer and healing. The handlers came by our sections, did not make eye contact, and kept moving.

None of the obviously disabled people were called up. No one prayed on the floor with any of us. No one acknowledged the sea of suffering gathered in this place. I don't know if the people brought on stage who said they had cancer or other ailments were healed. I don't doubt some were. I realized that if one of us had gone up on stage, it would have been very obvious whether our child was healed or not. But how good it would have been to receive prayer! When the time passed 11pm, we decided to leave. I touched the family in front of us, told them that I was witnessing a miracle as they took care of their child, and I spoke a prayer of blessing over them. I did not want the night's event to distract them from what God was already doing in their family.

A few years later, we had our second contact with faith healing. A man internationally known for raising someone from the dead came for a weekend at our church. He spoke to the leadership of the church in the afternoon, and a healing service was scheduled for later. We had Jillian with us and could not make the later service, so we went up and spoke with him when the leadership meeting was dismissed. As we talked with this gentleman, he looked directly at Jillian. He touched her. He then looked at Paul and me with compassion and sadness and grace. He said, "This is a very special child." He believed that total healing for Jillian would be difficult, and he encouraged us to pray for other miracles like her not having seizures or her being able to grow. He prayed boldly for her but not as if her healing was a sure thing. He prayed for Paul and me and for our family. He grieved with us. He saw who she was and celebrated her life. Paul and I left encouraged from this time. We had peace that God would heal her if that would bring Him glory. But right now Jillian was bringing Him glory in her chair.

Why does God allow us to suffer when He gets glory through healing? I wonder if today in modern America, where medicine, technology, and media rule the day, if people are not more impacted by those who suffer. We fear suffering and avoid it at all costs, and do not know what to do when it comes our way. A person or a family walking out a painful experience well draws attention and points people to God.

Chapter 5

Round 2: Bad Gets Worse

Age 7 through 9

Holy darkness, blessed night,
Heaven's answer hidden from our sight.
As we await you, O God of silence,
We embrace your holy night.

Catholic Hymn

For over thee years, Jillian had experienced peace. She slept better, gained weight, regained eye contact, and enjoyed life. We had become a functioning family regardless of having a child with special needs. The boys were thriving in elementary school, and I had recovered from the physically and emotionally draining season of Jillian's regression. After a wonderful year of kindergarten at Christ Presbyterian Academy, I met with the principal and the first-grade teachers to see if they had vision for Jillian continuing on. The group of students who knew her would be interspersed with the rest of the grade between three classes. As I explained to the three teachers who Jillian was and how she intersected with the other students, it became clear that all three teachers wanted the opportunity to have Jillian in their rooms so all the students could be with her! This was such a gift to me.

We decided to split her year equally between the first grade classrooms, and Jillian began in Deen Logan's room. Jane Carroll continued as her assistant, which provided continuity from the previous year. Jillian still enjoyed going, but deskwork did not hold her attention. Jane helped her by doing hand-over-hand writing or coloring, but Jillian seemed a little less content. Still Jane and Deen had many stories about how Jillian responded to her classmates and how they reached out to her. Her November birthday fell during her time in Deen's room. The children brought gifts and cards for Jillian and loved on her all day. This is a card I wrote to her teachers after her birthday:

> On Tuesday I went shopping for Jillian's birthday. I bought nothing and came away suddenly frustrated that she could use and do so little. I usually have a vision for her birthday, to celebrate who God has made her to be.

> This year I had no vision, no plan. I made cookies, which was a fun project, and prayed that they would bless her classmates. Cookies she can't eat. Part of my heart had an unexpected rekindle of grief and loss.
>
> Today I watched as God unfolded His birthday vision and plan for Jillian. You and your students were Jesus to my seven-year-old girl, and to me. When we brought her home, she smiled for hours! Thank you for drawing my eyes back to Jesus. He had abundantly provided for her again, as He always has. And she is a happy child, confident in His provision.
>
> I wanted you to know how much more today was than cookies and cards. In this mother's heart, it was a strong reminder that God is turning what was meant for evil into good.

Deen said later in a card to Jillian, "Our class was never finer than when we joined you in celebrating your 7th birthday!! We all lit up with pure joy over you!!" I heard from numerous parents the things their children told them about Jillian, and I loved to hear their perspective. One little girl told her mother they had to go shopping for Jillian's birthday. This six-year-old selected things Jillian could enjoy, including a festive warm hat and gloves and a stuffed teddy bear. Not only did a bridge exist between Jillian and the children, but also she created one between me and the other parents of her class.

In December, Jillian joined Susan Cline's classroom. Susan had been Luke's kindergarten teacher during Jillian's first regression, and she had a tremendous affection for Jillian. Again, school went well, but Jillian was sick several days and seemed fussy. Then in spring, she moved to the third teacher's room; she had only gone a few times when I volunteered to drive on a field trip so Jillian could go in our van. Several animated classmates climbed in, thrilled to ride in our conversion van, and fascinated with the electric lift and the tie downs used to secure her wheelchair. The drive to the children's theatre was happy, and I loved hearing the chatter going on around my silent child. At the theatre, however, Jillian didn't seem to pay attention and became more agitated.

The drive back to school was the opposite from the one there. Jillian strained and pushed, extending her now-rigid legs and arms, and began to cry out like she was in pain. These episodes were becoming more common at home, so I knew there was little I could do and she probably just had to get through it. But now the bouncy first graders were stone silent. I did my best to explain that she was fine, but sometimes her body did not serve her and she got frustrated. That seemed like the longest drive. After I dropped the other students off at school, I took Jillian home with me. At home I got her out of her chair and held her tight in bed till she calmed down. As I lay with her, I faced the reality of what I had been denying. She was getting worse again, and the periods of agitation were growing. More significant was the fact that her body was going into puberty early, and many Rett girls experience a second regression during puberty. She never went back to Christ Presbyterian Academy. I didn't make the decision immediately; it just seemed that each day was consumed with simply getting her through the day.

While I knew it was time to keep Jillian at home, we always felt part of her class at CPA. Over the years, parents often introduced themselves to me saying that their son or daughter was in Jillian's class. When Jillian died, the principal showed her peers, then in fifth grade, a video about her, and talked about her death, funeral, and new life with Jesus. The principal also thanked the class for loving her well when she attended school with them.

Children with special needs often go into puberty early because of their brain injury. Jillian was just seven years old, and I grieved the loss of childhood. She grew taller, became more detached, and unpredictably fussy. We homeschooled her exclusively and had caregivers with her every morning teaching educational material, doing a home therapy program, and simply being with her. As we were in control of her schedule, we could tailor it to fit her mood, sleepiness, and discomfort. Walking outside, playing music and moving her chair, and physical touch helped her reset during bad spells. This regression was not as severe as her first one as a toddler, and some days or hours she was present and happy. Many of the family trips I discussed earlier happened during this time, and we learned ways to get her comfortable. But when she was unhappy, she cried and wailed and sounded like something was very wrong.

Even though we knew that girls with Rett syndrome have second regressions causing fussiness, we could not just assume that we could do nothing for her apparent pain. What if she had pain from a physiological cause like gall stones or acid reflux and could not tell us? We worked with her seizure meds, adjusted her wheelchair, and consulted therapists. Nothing brought relief. She started waking up every night and either crying or staying awake for hours.

We took her to one of the best pediatric orthopedic surgeons in Nashville. He had helped train my husband at Vanderbilt Medical School and was legendary there. The doctor, a serious man who was not effusive, did a thorough evaluation for scoliosis, a common Rett complication. The exam found no scoliosis. He also looked at her hips to make sure her tight ligaments had not causes hip dislocation. I will never forget this excellent physician watching her writhe and cry on the table. "Something is really bothering her. We must find out what it is. Have you considered…?" For every diagnosis he suggested, we said we had pursued that line of thought. The three of us sat in the exam room confused and undone that we could not help her. His time, compassion, and effort did not make Jillian better, but it was a gift that he sat with us in that overwhelmed place for a few minutes. We felt an experienced doctor had seen her in pain, brainstormed with us, and left no stone unturned. All that remained was her hurt brain trying to grow in puberty and sending inappropriate pain and tone messages. Involuntary continuously contracted muscles, called spasticity, eventually cause deformities, and spasticity can draw muscles in or make them extend. Her increased muscle tone hurt her body, frustrated her, and wore her out.

During this season, Jillian had another status epilepticus episode, meaning she had an episode of continuous seizures. We took her to the hospital, where doctors tried unsuccessfully to stop the seizures with medicine. They were not severe seizures, just rhythmic jerking and a distant gaze, but the brain can be hurt if it seizes too long. It took about 24 hours to get the seizures under control. After a few days in the hospital, an unfamiliar neurologist came to see Jillian on morning rounds. Jillian lay apathetic and flaccid on the bed, not very responsive even for her. I was stressed, tired, and fearful of what would be left of Jillian after she recovered. The neurologist was not terribly personable, and I made the mistake of putting him in the position of God—I asked him a question to which only God knew the answer. We do that often with physicians, and it is unfair to them. Then we judge them when they give us a wrong answer. The wisest doctors answer "I don't know" to those kinds of questions. I asked this neurologist, "She seems so wiped-out after these few days. Will she continue like this or return to her previous baseline?" This was unfair because he did not know her, and really no one knew what brain damage, if any, had occurred. Instead of a "let's wait and see" answer, he looked at her coldly and said, "This is her new baseline." I felt like I had been slapped. At the same time, the Holy Spirit was speaking in my head, "Don't believe this—this is not true!" We had received so much bad news from doctors that had been true, and we had received it and not denied it. But this time I felt the Holy Spirit say a firm "No!" The neurologist said some other things I don't remember. I was grateful that God could speak either through or over doctors as He saw fit. I hoped I would never force a doctor into playing God again.

New medicines kept Jillian's seizures under control, and she was slowly coming out of her second regression. She seemed to get sick often, with drainage down her throat. We had a hard time telling whether this was true illness that could be treated or just a consequence of her inability to swallow correctly. Saliva pooled in her mouth, and because of her poor tone, she would cough or drool. Cycles of excessive mucus, coughing, choking, and discomfort dominated many of Jillian's days. We decided to have a CT scan of her sinuses, as they can become chronically infected and blocked. She did well for the test, and the radiologist called my husband, whom he knew, with the results. The radiologist seemed reserved or hesitant. He reported that Jillian's sinuses were clear, and then he paused. He asked what other imaging we had done on Jillian's brain. As a toddler she had a normal MRI, and we had not done any since.

Finally he came to the point: "The front part of her brain above her sinuses shows massive atrophy, like she was a drowning victim or had some other major trauma." Atrophy means to waste away or degenerate.

Paul was shocked and felt like he was hearing an autopsy report. Obviously, she had not had outward trauma to her brain, but it had atrophied on its own. Even though this news did not impact our care of Jillian, it was another loss. It offered a possible explanation for her moodiness as the front part of the brain controls memory and emotion. It also implied that she most likely had impaired cognition, not just motor disability. Up until this point I had not embraced any mental limitation diagnosis, as Rett syndrome primarily affects the girls' physical ability. When we shared the CT results with Jillian's Rett specialist, he said that about 50% of Rett girls develop some atrophy, usually in the front part of their brain. Another piece of our daughter was gone, Since no one knew why this degenerative process happened, we could assume it would continue to get worse. Paul and I grieved her loss, her suffering, and our inability to fix each new problem.

During this second regression and until the end of Jillian's life, her sleeping remained disrupted. We decided that her sleep-onset mechanism did not work correctly. Every night, we medicated her to fall asleep. Some nights the sedative did not affect her, and she cried and cried. She was tired, and her muscle tone would tighten, making her unable to relax. One night this happened while we were hosting a gathering of our closest friends and their families. There were over 30 people in our home. I had put Jillian to bed in her bedroom and was out serving food and enjoying the company. The house was full of the sound of older kids and conversation. I usually left Jillian for a while when I put her to bed to see if she would fall asleep.

That night, Jillian was fussing in her room, and I did not hear her. But several of my friends' daughters heard her. They were concerned and wanted to pray for her. My friend Angela was nearby and they went into Jillian's room and prayed. Jillian continued to cry, getting louder and more agitated. I finally heard her and came back to her room. I found the door open, the room still dark, and my friend and my daughter's friends praying for her. I thanked them and told them I needed to help her get to sleep by lying down with her, so they left. But Angela stayed. I lay next to Jillian, as I did many nights, my front to her back. I had my arm under her head and used my other arm to pull up her legs into a fetal position. By this time, Jillian was almost 70 pounds and had long, strong legs. She would involuntarily strain her hardest, keeping her legs taut and extended. I had to try to force her legs to bend. I always won after a struggle, and Jillian would cry out in sharp pain, nearly breaking my heart. And then she would relax into the fetal position, and her body would stop fighting. This night was the same. Jillian screamed out, then her body went slack. Soon she was asleep, and I wormed my way out of her bed, praying I did not wake her. This getting-to-sleep routine took twenty minutes, and Angela was there the whole time. When I got up, Angela was crying, and she hugged me. It struck me that no one had ever seen this except for Paul and the kids. I had told people that Jillian had sleep problems and that I had to help her get to sleep, but no one had ever seen what it involved. Angela witnessed an intimate and painful part of our daily life, and stood in that place of raw compassion with me.

Many girls with Rett syndrome reach the end of their second regression and have a new season of peace, which can last well into adulthood. Jillian's mood did stabilize and the periods of screaming did diminish, but her physical difficulties continued to progress. I felt like we had weathered her second regression well: adapting her schedule to maximize her good days, grieving losses while enjoying what we had of her, dealing with health crises without sacrificing rich family experiences. The truths God had shown us about suffering played out in the arena of her regression. He startled and amazed us with His provision. Most of these provisions disappeared from my memory like manna, forcing me to look for fresh provision again and again. But some stories, like of her seventh birthday at CPA, stand out like Ebenezers in the history of my life with God.

The family in Colorado, Jillian is nine.

Jillian on a camping trip, reading with Dad, and celebrating her birthday with a cheesecake.

Jillian laughing at a wind chime, playing the marimba with her Grandma, chilling in her beanbag chair, and joined by her siblings in wheelchairs at a science museum.

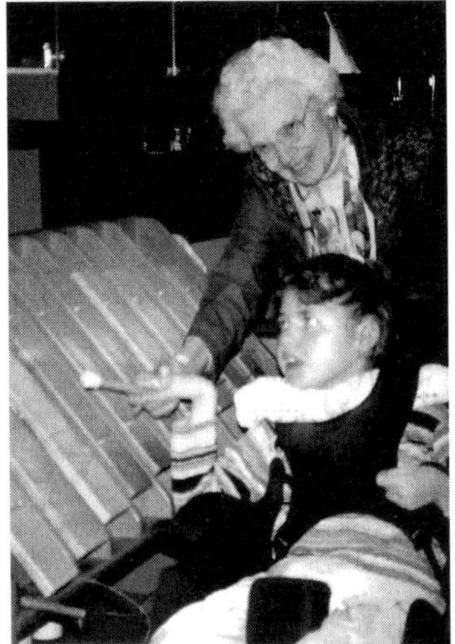

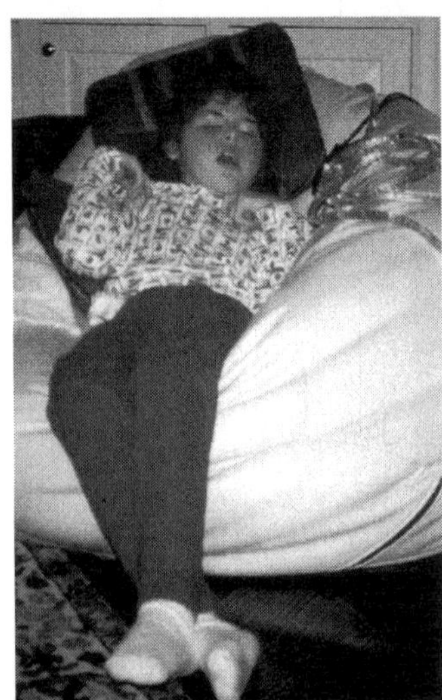

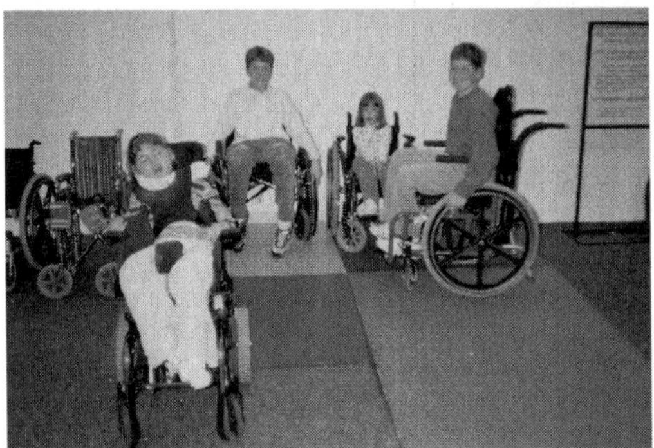

Chapter 6

Finishing Well

Age 10 through 11

The question is not: What can I do in the years I have left? But: what must I do to make my last and eternal days fruitful? We all push aside the thought of dying. No; it's most important to prepare for death. Getting older is also a form of dying. You can't do this. You can't do that. Jesus told us about the grain of corn. It has to die, otherwise it won't bear fruit. We are always dying. The question is: Are we able to make death a fruitful gift? I'm always asking myself: How can I prepare myself for death, so my death bears fruit?

Henri Nouwen
from the movie *Christian Catalyst Collection: Henri Nouwen*

Truly I tell you, unless a kernel of wheat falls to the ground and dies, it remains only a single seed. But if it dies, it produces many seeds.
John 12:24 (NIV)

Now that Jillian had come through her second regression and could return to school, we had to decide where she should go. Since she would now be in third grade, which required more seatwork, I felt that her time at Christ Presbyterian Academy had ended. I had also read an article in *Exceptional Parent Magazine* written by an adult with physical disabilities who had always been mainstreamed in regular elementary and middle schools. While he had appreciated the opportunities he had experienced, he had felt alone and different. When he got to high school, he finally met other students with disabilities and realized the camaraderie he had missed all those years. It struck me that Jillian had never been around other disabled children in any setting! She attended a regular school or school at home for the first nine years of her life—which had been good—but I wondered if she would enjoy the companionship of others who knew what she went through every day.

Our first experience with this was at an Easter Seals camp about forty-five minutes from our home. This overnight camp had a high staff-student ratio and served a wide variety of children with special needs. Jillian required extensive medical and physical support at night, making her unable to attend, but I knew she could access the daytime activities. At the same time, Paul and I had been looking for an opportunity for our family to be involved in community service. We missed our times in Ecuador because they stretched us beyond our natural abilities. We realized that we were well qualified to take care of kids with special needs. Even our boys, now 10 and 12, could push wheelchairs and assist anyone needing help to participate in activities. Our daughter Rachel, age three, simply brought the gift of joy and was not fazed by anyone who walked or talked a little differently. We spoke with the camp director and volunteered to help for the week they had kids like Jillian.

Jillian had her own group and counselor, and we helped around the camp in different areas, taking her home with us each night. Paul drove the pontoon boat and repaired the dock in his spare time. Luke and Andrew helped on the archery range, drove the golf cart to fill up water coolers, built the campfires, and cleaned up. I staffed the arts and crafts room with Rachel. At first I struggled to let "strangers" take care of Jillian, but they soon became friends, and we learned much from them.

Jillian was paired with another camper who could walk, and I remember the tenderness and care this adolescent girl with special needs took in pushing Jillian or making sure she could participate. I enjoyed doing arts and crafts with kids of all ages and abilities. The focus was process, not accomplishment, and most students found ways to express themselves creatively. That experience helped me look to the future with Jillian and see that she could benefit from being in a special needs environment. She did not need to be totally dependent on me to access life. Her counselor and other staff brought valuable knowledge and personality traits to her life, and the other campers became her friends.

My favorite family story from camp occurred one day at lunchtime. The campers ate lunch in a big indoor pavilion. Cafeteria-style meals meant campers ate as groups with their counselor. Jillian was tube-fed so she just enjoyed the lunchtime activity, but we were hungry. The first day we ate lunch, our table included a girl who could feed herself, but much of her lunch (and a lot of drool) ended up back on her plate. She patiently worked at it, but it was not pretty. Another camper at our table periodically screamed—not in pain—but randomly and loudly. Each table repeated the scenes of brokenness in the context of eating. I looked around, distracted and suddenly not very hungry. Then I watched our boys. They were digging into lunch with gusto, asking for someone to pass the rolls. They looked around content and happy, oblivious to the oral and auditory chaos around them. I was amazed, then convicted of my own discomfort, and then grateful that my sons had learned from Jillian to be at ease around these children. I sat down and tucked in to my delicious fried bologna!

Jillian's experience at camp gave me confidence to consider placing her in a school for children with special needs that fall. Her body was bigger now—about 75 pounds—and I felt like she needed more support and services than I could provide at home. Again I visited Harris Hillman, the Nashville school that serves children with multiple disabilities. At that time Harris Hillman focused primarily on physical positioning (getting students out of wheelchairs into different positions in standers, side-lying tables, swings, and bean bags); providing a stimulating environment with toys, lights, and music; and offering adaptive programs for PE, music, art and computer. Paul and I met with the principal and toured the facility. The staff listened to us well, and the brightness and friendliness of the campus impressed us. I wanted Jillian to have an assistant on the bus, because she choked frequently on her secretions. The school department said they would provide an assistant for us. Suddenly, our child would be getting up, catching a bus, and leaving me until they brought her home at 3:30! I felt it would be good for her and me to have this new level of independence, and both the bus driver and assistant were dedicated to Jillian and the other students. Many who choose to work with children with special needs are not only comfortable with health and behavior challenges, but draw joy and significance from serving those others might consider "broken." They see the hidden strengths of weakness.

Because I had free time now, and I wanted to stay involved with Jillian's schooling, I joined the PTA and volunteered to start a newsletter. This allowed me to go where I wanted in the building, interview staff and parents, and learn more about special education in Nashville. The school is built with open pods connected to a central cafeteria. Classrooms have no doors, and staff welcome visitors. Many local high schools and colleges send students to help at Harris Hillman. I was welcomed wherever I wanted to help. Soon teachers, parents, and staff became my friends as we planned fundraisers and organized parent support groups. Not only did Jillian have a peer group that joined in her journey, but also for the first time I had friends who understood my journey as a parent and caregiver. Luke, Andrew, and Rachel also became involved. Luke participated in "Sibling Day" and spent the day at school with Jillian. Rachel played her violin for several classrooms. Later Andrew would be a volunteer counselor for their summer program. My children learned to receive the blessing of brokenness from the other students also. They looked passed outward disabilities to the vibrant, often mischievous, and nonjudgmental personalities of Jillian and her peers.

Also during this last season, Jillian and I took a special trip. Paul had taken each of our boys on a trip when they turned 13. The idea was to acknowledge that our sons were transitioning and each beginning his journey toward manhood. Paul planned fun trips and read a book with each of them that talked about growing into men. The fall of Jillian's 10th year, I had the opportunity to take her on her own trip to Toronto. In the last season of his life, Henri Nouwen learned the importance of ministering to the broken through his time at Daybreak, a handicapped community in Toronto. This is the story of my taking Jillian to Daybreak.

Several years earlier, one of the people God provided to help me with Jillian was Jennifer Martin, a singer, songwriter, worship leader, and (now) episcopal priest here in Nashville. We attended the same church and had met several times through mutual friends. At a time when I had been praying for more help with Jillian, Jennifer called me out of the blue and said she thought God wanted her to spend time with people in wheelchairs. She called me for direction, but when I expressed my need, she decided to start with Jillian (she later got to hang out with many others in wheelchairs including my mother). So Jennifer started coming to my home once or twice a week to spend time with Jillian. They often sat together at the piano while Jennifer sang. They danced in our family room, Jennifer pushing and twirling the chair. They went outside with Jennifer's guitar. Jennifer is also trained in massage, and she gave massage therapy to Jillian, helping her tight muscles. One day while Jillian sat in her wheelchair next to Jennifer at the piano, Jennifer wrote a song called "The Lame Can Dance." She says she co-wrote it with Jillian. The lyrics are:

> I want to dance with you, spin with you, love on you always.
> I want the world to know what I have found in your arms.
> See I am free in you, clean in you, whole, though I am broken.
> Witness the miracle—See! The lame can dance.
>
> Come dance! All who are weary, come dance—
> All who are mourning, come dance,
> All the wounded and broken.

Come dance, all who are needy, come dance—
He's extending his hand to you to dance.

Beauty for ashes, the peace that surpasses all seasons—
You take my pieces, my weakness, and give me your strength.
In place of rejection, you lavish affection upon me.
Join in the miracle—See! The lame can dance.

I'm finally learning the rhythm of grace as you lead me.
Loving you, trusting you more each time we dance.
Sing to me, flow through me,
  show me the movement of mercy.
I'm living proof to the world: the lame can dance.[1]

Jennifer took this song with her as she traveled to worship conferences at churches around the country and world. She told people about Jillian and sang the song and invited all who were broken to come to Jesus and dance. Many people identified with the song, including a woman who had been recently diagnosed with terminal cancer. Jennifer maintained a relationship with this woman until her death. The message of dancing with Jesus despite our brokenness had universal appeal, as we are all broken in some way. Jennifer recorded the song in Nashville as part of a worship project. Later, we asked a videographer to come film Jillian and our family. Snapshots of Jillian were usually unflattering, but a video captured her peaceful, feminine grace. The videographer spent several hours filming her and us, in and out of our home. Then he and Jennifer edited the footage and put it to "The Lame Can Dance." A treasure when it was made, this video has only become more valuable with time.

As part of her worshiping arts ministry, Jennifer was asked to participate in a Catholic women's worship project. This gathered ten young women who ministered throughout the county in different Catholic Church venues, bringing contemporary worship to congregations. As the artists spent time together during the recording process, they shared their music. Jennifer played "The Lame Can Dance." One artist, Susan HooKong-Taylor, lived near Daybreak in Toronto, and often participated in worship at the L'Arche center. Daybreak had a dance group of community members called Spirit Movers, headed by a woman named Kathy Kelly. After hearing the song and the story of Jennifer and Jillian's friendship, Kathy invited us to come to Toronto and be a part of a dance concert that would feature Susan, Spirit Movers, and "The Lame can Dance."

So Jennifer, Jillian, and I packed into our conversion van and drove to Toronto. While Jennifer stayed with Susan, Jillian and I stayed in the house where Henri Nouwen had lived and served. In the basement was the chapel where he administered Communion to community members. The library and kitchen were as they had been when Henri lived there. The lane outside that connected the house with the community was bright with purple flowers and songbirds. I couldn't believe I was there with my daughter. We spent several days in the community. We ate in a house where adults with special needs live together with assistants. We met community members, practiced with the dance team, and even made a video of our story for *Salt and Light*, a Catholic television channel. In one of the dance rehearsals, we showed the team how we pushed Jillian in her wheelchair from one of us to the other as part of dancing and how she smiled. It could be quite gracefully done. So walking members of the dance team tried pushing wheelchair-bound members, or twirling them. It was beautiful, and the people in the wheelchairs loved it. The time culminated with an evening dance where the larger Toronto community was invited to see the Daybreak dance group and hear Jennifer and Susan. The lovely, holy evening ended with "The Lame Can Dance. "

The next day we left, very full from our time, and drove home via Niagara Falls. We got to the falls around lunchtime. The parking lot was packed, and as I got out Jillian's seizure pills to grind up, I laughed and thought: "I bet I am the only person in this huge parking lot with a mortar and pestle in my car." But we were here! We pushed up to the top of the falls. Jillian could feel the spray and hear the roar, but the walls were understandably too high for her to see over. So we went in the Table Rock Restaurant and they gave us a seat by the huge window. We carried her chair down a few steps to get there, and Jillian had a great view of the falls. Back at home I tangibly felt the love of God who had orchestrated this appropriate, accessible, and affirming trip

As Christmas approached, Jillian's health continued to decline. We tried injections of botox into her constantly straining muscles, which were painful and brought no relief. She could not manage her secretions well, and they pooled in the back of her throat, causing coughing and choking. Frequent suctioning was only mildly effective, and we contemplated getting her salivary glands removed to bring her relief. Another loss. She had one sinus infection after another. The skin over the bony parts of her body occasionally got the beginnings of bedsores. Her sleep remained poor, even with medication. Her digestive tract did not work correctly, and her bowel movements were increasingly uncomfortable. Every week brought more problems than answers.

One day, the physical therapist at Jillian's school asked if Jillian could be a patient at a local conference for training new therapists. I agreed and didn't think anything about it until I arrived with her at the venue. I had to take her out of her chair and lay her on a table in front of a room of 50 therapists. I am very supportive of medical education and was happy to have her be a part of clinical diagnosis and treatment. But as they talked about her and about things that had or had not been done or could be done, seeing her long body with her straining legs sticking up, I became emotional and could not wait to leave.

I cried and cried in the van on the way home. I was surprised at my excessive emotion and tried to work through it. Jillian was becoming more trapped in her own body and less happy. We put her on oral baclofen, which reduces muscle tone, and it worked. She sat quietly in her chair, but now everything was still and she just moved her eyes. Purposeful motion disappeared. The secretions worsened, and she spent a lot of time coughing. I pictured her physical body as a leaky roof that we kept sticking buckets under and trying to patch. Now this roof had more holes than solid structure, and we were running around in a panic since each solution caused more problems. On that drive home, I realized that over the previous month or so, I had been unable to see a path to escape from Jillian's growing problems. For the first time I was afraid for her future.

In the midst of my growing anxiety over Jillian's future and my fatigue as a caregiver, Paul suggested we get a dog. Andrew had been asking for a puppy for years. This seemed like insanity to me, but my husband felt strongly that we would lose the window of time for Andrew to enjoy a dog if we waited until things were easier. He would be off to college before we knew it. Taking care of that new puppy nearly put me over the edge! Fortunately Paul spent much time training the dog with the boys. Sometimes I took the puppy, Jit, back with me to get Jillian ready for school. I would put Jit on Jillian's bed while I changed Jillian's diaper and clothes, and that active, rambunctious puppy would lie still without a word from me. What could this young dog know about Jillian that caused her to be peaceful? Jillian died a month after we brought home the puppy, and I was so grateful that we had a puppy in the house during that season.

That Christmas, with the puppy in our arms, we drove to Pittsburgh to be with my mother and entire extended family. My mother continued to wrestle with her own disabilities from rheumatoid arthritis and growing blindness. I showed my mother, my siblings, and their children the video made about our visit to Toronto. I also showed them parts of videos I had purchased at Daybreak, including one about Henri Nouwen.

As he talked in the video about his life with Adam, the severely disabled man in the community home, Nouwen said, "Adam affected everyone in the home. And how we treated him also affected us. If Adam was not doing well, we were not doing well. He called us beyond ourselves."

This truth bore out in our immediate family. As we all extended ourselves to care for Jillian, we rose above our own natural selfishness and our family community benefited. Our extended family lived far away from us and did not see our daily lives with Jillian. These videos allowed us to share Jillian and her transforming work with them. I still have the picture in my mind of the evening when we watched these videos together, watching Jillian in Toronto and hearing Henri's powerful words in community with Adam. My handicapped mother sat in her power recliner watching too, and fell asleep. Like Henri with Adam, or the five of us with Jillian, my extended family did best as we came around my mother in her disabilities. She called us beyond ourselves also.

As good as I felt about Toronto and Christmas with my family, my worry over Jillian grew. I often wondered if she could continue living in her current condition. I thought about her dying. This was not a new thought. Over the last five years of Jillian's life, I walked at the nearby lake each week and prayed, thought, and tried to hear God. I felt like Jillian would probably die young. Dr. Percy, our Rett specialist, had said that Jillian had major risk factors for early death: immobility, seizures, and low muscle tone. It seemed that swallowing difficulty could have been added to the list. Whenever we turned a rough corner in our medical journey with Jillian, I always planned her funeral in my mind. I felt guilty about this until I read about another Rett mom who did this. There were so many losses along the way, and every time my mother's heart grieved. These "funerals" were much sadder for me than her final one.

Every month, the IRSF newsletter shared obituaries of girls who had died—many in their sleep of a heart arrhythmia, pneumonia, or breathing issues. I started thinking that I needed to prepare our family for the possibility of Jillian's dying young. This may sound morbid, and I think it is outside much Protestant thinking, but I decided to study some Catholic material about "dying well." This was instructive for me as a person, independent of Jillian. I needed to confront mortality so I could live with no regrets. One author discussed the concept of praying for a good death. We pray for good days, good births, good trips, why not pray for a good death?

I wanted Jillian to have as full a life as she could while she had it, and for us not to be taken off-guard if she died young. So I prayed that all her work here on earth would be accomplished, and that I would take care of her. I then prayed hard that she would just slip away during the night since many Rett girls do. I prayed that it would be easy for her, that we would be ready, and that God would receive glory from her life. It seemed the best of many options. I didn't want her to live long in her uncooperative body, and at times when she was unhappy for long periods, I wanted her released. At other times when she was at peace, I felt I could push her wheelchair for decades!

And one day, suddenly, it happened. On Thursday night, January 20, 2005, I put Jillian to bed and for the first time all week she smiled at me. During the night she had odd breathing, different than I had ever heard. I checked on her in bed, and she didn't have any other symptoms: no fever, no elevated heart rate, no distress. I did wake Paul to talk with him about it, and I talked to God about it as I always did when I got up with Jillian at night. I cleared my mind, prayed, and tried to pause and listen for any inner voice. Paul reminded me Jillian had no symptoms to treat, so we let her rest. On Friday morning she had mild fever, but her breathing was normal. I kept her home from school, and all day she lay in bed and drowsed. My mind started sorting through the possibilities of what could be wrong. Since she could not tell me, I needed to make good observations and decide when to involve her doctor. Paul listened to her that night, but she still had no symptoms that demanded medical attention. Friday night I woke up and checked on her. She had fever again, but her pulse and breathing were normal. I treated her fever and lay back down and prayed. What do I do? And I felt in my head the word "Sleep!" In all the years of being up with Jillian and talking to God in the night, I had not ever heard that direction. And so I tried to be obedient to that voice, and I had peace and did fall asleep.

The next morning she looked sick to me, like a child with fever. We decided to ask our pediatrician, Dr. Bill Long, to see her just in case we were missing something. Before he got to our house, I called two of my closest friends and asked them to pray that the doctor would have wisdom to know what to do. Because that was the real issue with Jillian: not how we could make her totally better, since we couldn't, but what next step could we take at this junction. Dr. Long evaluated her early that morning, and she still had no alarming features; her lungs sounded fine, her fever was low, and her other vital signs were within normal range. Dr. Long decided we would put her on antibiotics as she had chronic sinus infections, and he came up with a plan should Jillian get worse. We could take her into the clinic or to the hospital if anything changed. Paul and I both felt great peace that this was the correct plan. A friend took five-year-old Rachel for the day. Luke, now in ninth grade, was already at a friend's house. Paul rounded on his patients in the hospital, and I got Jillian's antibiotic. She was the same—resting and quiet.

Paul came home and we had a peaceful lunch, coming up with our strategy for the day and how best to take care of our family. Andrew, our seventh grader, was sitting on the couch and at the end of our lunchtime said, "Mom, Jill's breathing sounds funny." We ran in and she was blue and gasping and lethargic and unable to cough. Since we had a plan, we knew what to do, and it was not a crazy scene. Andrew saw how sick she was. He collected things to take to a friend's house and to care for his puppy. I drove our big conversion van while Paul sat in the back of this "ambulance" with Jill in his arms. He sang to her and she roused and smiled in spite of her blueness. We prayed and asked God to streamline things at the hospital and again to facilitate her care. Paul said, "What if they need to resuscitate her?" We decided, as we had discussed in the past, that if she had something treatable, then we should support her recovery.

The most poignant scene from that day is Paul carrying a blue Jillian to the ambulance doors of the emergency department. They were locked and he pounded on them, and two doctors with white coats streaming came running down the hall to open the doors, and then ushered Paul in with great haste. I parked the van and called Luke so he would know how sick she was and that she might have to be intubated. When I got into the Emergency Department, Paul greeted me with relief on his face: Jillian had responded to an oxygen mask and regained her normal color. The ER doctor was a good friend of Paul's, and Dr. Long showed up right after we got there. We went in her room together and she was alert and moving her head, resisting the nasal oxygen they were placing on her face. I talked to her and reassured her, holding her hand.

The doctors, including Paul, all left the room to look at her chest X-Ray. Maybe she did have some mild pneumonia? They pointed and looked at the film, as it was not obvious. I was alone in the room with Jillian and suddenly her heart rate began to drop. I went to the door to find Paul. Jillian was peaceful on the bed, but the alarm sounded on the heart monitor. The doctors all rushed back in and gave her an injection that brought up her heart rate. Quickly they tried to figure out why her heart rate was falling, because it immediately started down again. They discovered that her heart had developed an arrhythmia—an unstable pattern of beating—and their only hope was to get it back to a normal rhythm. The attending physician from the Pediatric Intensive Care Unit arrived to run the resuscitation. Every time they gave her an injection, her heart rate would go up (although not as high each time), and they had several minutes for the next attempt to fix her arrhythmia. The doctors moved quickly, and the room filled with activity as they intubated Jillian and sedated her. I talked to her as she fell asleep. They called for an echo machine to ultrasound her heart, and the tech who brought it in the room was a member of my church! My heart leapt and I motioned for her to pray for us as she left. She nodded and I felt God reassuring me that He knew what was going on.

As I stood there it seemed so ironic, almost cruel, that Paul, a certified resuscitation instructor, had to watch a resuscitation play out on his child. But I really believe God orchestrated it all this way. Everything unfolded peacefully, although it progressed to a negative outcome. The PICU doctor counseled with us after each attempt to fix her arrhythmia failed. He showed Paul a paper EKG strip like a long grocery receipt that showed Jillian's heart getting weaker and weaker. The path became clear. *Her heart is going...her heart will not recover...it is not about her lungs...there is nothing we can do...it is her time...let her go.* The actual death seemed small. Just a full cup of water edging toward cresting and then it slips over the edge.

The Emergency Department allowed us to stay in Jillian's room with her body for several hours. Almost everyone who loved her came in to say goodbye. Our friends brought our other children. Luke held her hand, normally drawn up and tight, now open and relaxed. He cried with sadness and joy, seeing her hand as a sign that she was free. Andrew, who always dreaded her death and cried whenever she got sick, said that it wasn't as bad as he thought it would be. What an important life lesson. Rachel sat in Paul's lap, surrounded by our friends and asked candid, innocent questions about death and heaven. After a few minutes, she quietly brought over a chair so she could climb up next to Jillian and drape herself across Jillian's body.

I had always been so grateful that I was not in charge of choreographing Jillian's death. I knew that God would be faithful to her, but I also knew that the journey could be rough. As I look back on the whole thing, I see His hand on the day, and I have such peace. Even though I knew she was sick, I can't go back to any point and say, "Oh, we missed it there" or "we ignored that" or "this would have changed it." And since we have always known that we would face this event, it seems like the best journey for her, even though the end was death. Paul and I experienced both closure and partnership being with her when she died, knowing she received the best medical care possible. Our medical community, church community, and school community came up under us before, during, and after her death, and we were not alone. More profoundly, our child's fight with her contracting body was over, and Jillian, the pure in heart, could see God.

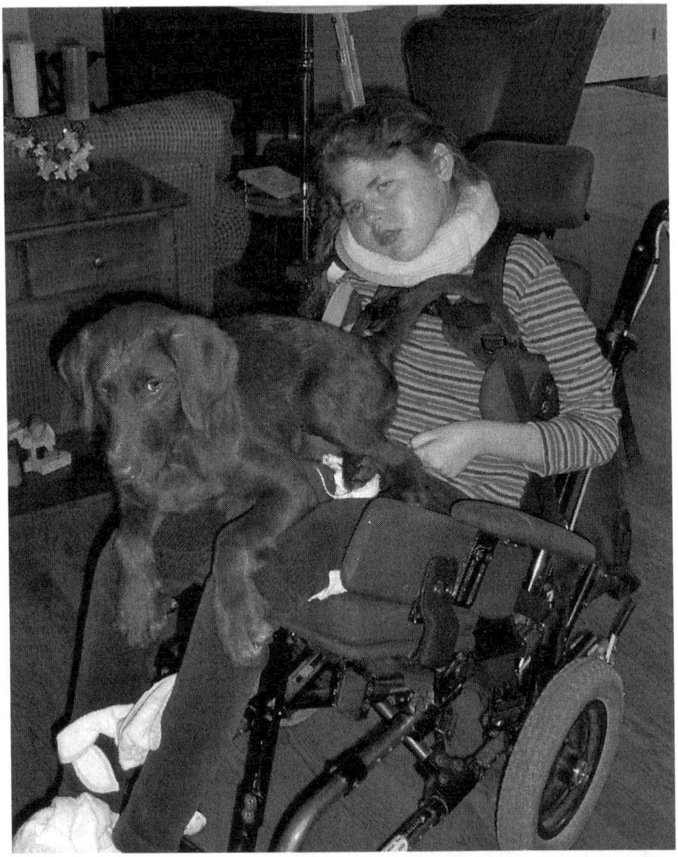

The last picture I took of Jillian, with our puppy, and her last formal portrait.

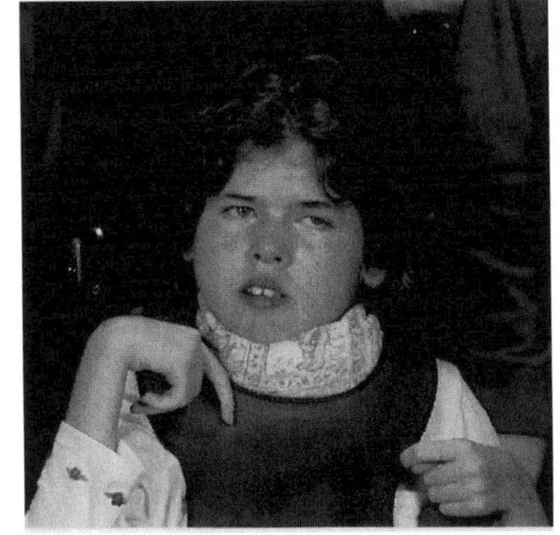

Chapter 7

The Funeral

Celebrating Her Life

Jillian Eileen Heil

November 19, 1993 – January 22, 2005

Just as I was writing these words, my canary burst forth with a song so joyous that a song was put also into my mouth. Something seemed to say, this captive sings in his cage because it has never known liberty, and cannot regret a lost freedom. So the soul of my child, limited by the restrictions of a feeble body, never having known the gladness of exuberant health, may sing songs that will enliven and cheer. Yes, and does sing them! What should we do without her gentle, loving presence, whose frailty calls forth our tenderest affections and whose sweet face makes sunshine in the shadiest places! I am sure that the boys are truly blessed by having a sister always at home to welcome them, and that their best manliness is appealed to by her helplessness. What this child is to me I cannot tell. And yet, if the skillful and kind Gardener should house this delicate plant before frosts come, should I dare to complain?

Mrs. E. Prentiss, *Stepping Heavenward*

The morning of Jillian's funeral, Paul and I dressed her body. It was such a familiar process that it was comforting rather than sad. The mortician warned us that seeing a body could be emotional and leave the family member with a negative picture. For us, the experience brought closure. We did not embalm her body, feeling it had been through enough. Seeing her again after the circumstances of her death allowed us to mourn, like the elephants with caressing trunks that return to the fallen body of a herd member. We selected a simple pine casket and dressed her in a favorite outfit, combing out her gorgeous hair. We put a teddy bear and a few other things with her. Her body would not be at the church for the service. Instead, her empty wheelchair stood at the front. We had the visitation before the service and greeted so many who loved her and us. Our friends Chris and Leslie Norton, who had performed at her birthday concert six years earlier, along with Jennifer Martin, provided music before and during the service. Once the memorial service started, Paul shared Max Lucado's quote about the old sweater in his closet. After showing the video of Jillian set to "The Lame Can Dance," Jennifer also spoke this eulogy:

> I got to hang out with Jillian a couple of mornings a week over a two-year period, doing a little massage therapy and a lot of worship music. In that time, I got to know Jill not only as this beautiful, red-haired girl in a wheelchair, but also as a special friend, a worshiper extraordinaire, as a dancer and a choreographer, as a songwriter, and a minister.
>
> "Preach the Gospel at all times, and when necessary use words." This is a phrase attributed to St. Francis of

Assisi. I attribute it to Jillian Heil—because, without opening her mouth, Jillian preached the Gospel of an upside down Kingdom in Christ Jesus—where "the poor are rich" and "the weak are strong," and "the lame can dance". And she did it all without ever saying a word.

And yet, sometimes, there would be words. As a music missionary, there were times, when I was out in the field, I would feel the Holy Spirit's prompting here and there: in this community, with that person, with this worship team, in so many places, to share Jillian's message, to share her song, to tell the Gospel Jillian preached every day without saying a word.

When I stopped to make phone calls and send emails on Saturday night, to tell people whom Jill had affected and ministered to over the last three years that she was now dancing in Heaven, I realized I was contacting people in over ten states and over four different nations.

To tell Jillian's story was to see other people find a safe place of love and acceptance to identify with their own brokenness, their own weakness, and in the mystery of the cross, find wholeness and joy and peace, not instead of their suffering, but in the *midst of* it.

Jillian, though captive in her own body, was a conduit through which the Holy Spirit moved beautifully and lovingly. And over the last three years, I witnessed Jillian's ministry set many a captive free. From personal experience, I can say with all gratitude; she did this very, very well.

Then I followed with my eulogy, which started:

One broken little girl, and here we all are. Thank you for coming tonight and honoring Jillian with your presence. We appreciate all of you and the community you have been to Jillian and to our family. We know that over the years you have prayed for her, cried with us, and seen glimpses of her special beauty and personality. Our family and Jillian's very life have been upheld by your prayers. And it was a good life.

Jillian was, despite her severe limitations, a happy person. This was not because her brain was too injured to know that she was suffering. Whenever we accidentally bonked her head lifting her into the van she cried out like you or I would. These cries were a great comfort to us, because we knew then that most of the time she was content. And even when she was having a difficult season of sleeping or illness, she would be upset, but never grouchy or belligerent or angry. A friend said to me once, "Jillian has learned the secret of being content in all situations," like Paul talks about in the Bible, and my friend added, "It is a secret, you know!" Jillian taught me some of that secret. She showed me how to live in the present, to enjoy the small things, and to not see negative circumstances as dead ends.

Jillian seemed very secure in who she was. I never felt she carried the burden of self-consciousness. She was glad to be included, yet not rejected when she was excluded. She received intimate care from friends as well as strangers without complaint, although it seemed that she would be more responsive with those she knew. She enjoyed her role in the family, being raced down the street by Andrew, ridden on by Rachel, lifted into bed by Luke, without feeling herself to be a bother, or a drain or a heavy load. She smiled with delight at the edge of the Grand Canyon, at the headwaters of the Colorado River, and the top of Clingman's Dome (all of which have paved trails). She was not robbed by not being able to hike the trail down the canyon, not riding the white waters of the Colorado, or by the thick cloud cover blocking any view in the Smokies. In fact, she did not let her disability rob her of life. She found life all around her and enjoyed it to the full. We always said, "Jillian's just glad to be along."

Jillian was a beautiful child. The distortion of her physical body, her drool or cough, and her wheelchair never took her beauty away. We were always so grateful for her flowing auburn hair because it gave strangers in elevators something to talk about. Her hands were soft and long-fingered. Her body smelled sweet and feminine. Her smile, though often hard to catch, was a gift to us. She loved to swim. In the summer, when I started to put on her bathing suit, she would smile her biggest smiles. And when we walked her into the pool, she would laugh out loud. The boys would swim under her and blow bubbles. Paul would play one-armed water basketball with her in the other arm. We called Jillian his handicap so the boys could have a chance to win. And Jillian would laugh and throw her head back when Rachel would slide down the slide and splash her in the face. I wonder if I will miss her in the pool the most. She was so easy to hold in the water, and she was so beautiful.

I went on to detail the history of the communities God had provided for Jillian to be loved including Judson Baptist preschool, elementary at CPA, Harris Hillman School, all the caregivers in our home, and our church family. As I spoke, the faces looking back at me from the congregation represented the vast and beautiful tapestry of Jillian's life network. I finished by talking briefly about the support from the medical community and her actual death:

> Vanderbilt Children's Hospital graciously provided care in routine appointments and in crises like on Saturday. Normally, resuscitation in an emergency room can be chaotic and threatening. But Saturday was a medical ballet, as Paul called it. Peaceful in the midst of intense activity, everything unfolding, Paul and I watching from the side—we were allowed to be part of the process which helped us let her go.
>
> Jillian, the Lord gave you to us all, and the Lord has taken you away from us, and we can truly say that God has been very good to us. We will miss you.

After that, Kristina Owen, who had cared for Jillian as a toddler on up, performed a dance she had choreographed to Chris Rice's "Untitled Hymn." With each verse Kristina acted out more elements of our lives and Jillian's life using the empty wheelchair. The final verse is:

And with your final heartbeat
Kiss the world goodbye
Then go in peace, and laugh on glory's side, and
Fly to Jesus, Fly to Jesus
Fly to Jesus and live[1]

On "Kiss the world goodbye," Kristina pushed the wheelchair away and danced in joyful circles at the front of the church. The painful and positive images in this performance summarized Jillian's life better than many words.

Doug and Dabney Mann, the mature couple who had walked with us through Jillian's diagnosis and early life each spoke about Jillian, addressing our other children and commending them for being caring siblings. Later, Don Finto, our pastor since our college days, shared this story as part of his closing prayer and benediction:

> About a year ago, Martha and I were eating lunch at a restaurant here in town, and it was the strangest thing; there was a family sitting in the corner, over away from us, and it was the strangest thing…I couldn't stop going back to them. I couldn't help it. I was drawn to them, and I thought, "This is so strange. Why do I keep looking at that family? What is different about that family? I can't keep my eyes off of them. I'm almost embarrassed, the way I keep looking at them." And then I thought, "OK, it's the way they are responding to each other. Something about the way they are reacting and relating to each other: it is so precious." Mother, father and three children. And when they got up and started to leave, I noticed that the girl who had her back to me was mentally challenged. I got up and went over to see the family. I told them what had been happening to me. And I said, "I know you wouldn't have chosen this, but let me tell you something. It has produced something so beautiful in your family, the way you relate to each other."

> Because, you see, I had just been reading out of Paul's Romans 5, where he gives what I call *God's Character Development Plan.* He says that since we are justified by faith, we have peace with God through our Lord Jesus Christ, by whom we also have access by faith into this grace in which we stand; and we rejoice in the hope of the glory of God. That's the foundation, but not only that, we rejoice in our suffering because—see, you can only do that in the Lord—we rejoice in our suffering because suffering produces perseverance, and perseverance, character. You don't get it any other way.

The next day, we buried Jillian in a memorial garden outside of Nashville. Our family and close friends attended the graveside service, and several people spoke of how Jillian had impacted them. I was grateful for the beautiful day that drew our eyes to the surrounding hills and up to the blue sky. On her grave marker, under her name, we put "The Lame will Dance."

Richard Anderson, Christ Presbyterian Academy headmaster, wrote a weekly column in the school newsletter. This is part of what he wrote about the day Jillian died:

> Emotions—and life itself—can "turn on a dime." They can change in the twinkling of an eye.
>
> This was brought home on Jan. 22.

He explained how that Saturday he and his wife Cindy (Jillian's former kindergarten teacher) were out of town when they got a call:

> At 5:00pm I was turning onto the exit for Birmingham International Airport. Cindy's cell phone rang. The news was not good—Jillian Heil, 11-year-old daughter of CPA parents Paul and Joyce Heil, had passed away around 3:30pm at Vanderbilt Hospital. Jillian was a child with special needs—a genetic disorder confined her to a wheelchair for the past few years.
>
> But Jillian's spirit was not confined to the wheelchair. Though she never attended school here, she was on campus often—she especially came alive when able to worship with the kindergarten class. Those little children loved her—the ministry was indeed "two-way." She knew how to worship.

He went on to describe Jillian's time in L'Arche Daybreak, dancing with the community members in her wheelchair. He continued:

> We pass a house every day on our way to school. Above the garage door is a neon sign. It simply says, "Welcome Home." I know nothing about the family who lives there—except that they must be loving.
>
> Sitting in the airport in Birmingham, I thought about that sign. And I thought about Jesus—arms outstretched—saying to Jillian, "Welcome Home." Jillian is dancing in the Kingdom now. One day we will, too...

After the funeral I looked in the backyard at our big cedar tree. It stood at least fifty feet tall, and instead of having one main trunk, it split into four parts about ten feet above the ground. Right before Jillian died, we came home to find one of the four trunks broken and lying on the lawn. As I looked at the tree, it reminded me of my four children, with one gone. That night, I wrote in her old baby journal book, "the prophetic image of the cedar with its four parts, one on the ground. The break leaves a scar but shows the heartwood of the tree."

Chapter 8

The Final Chapter

Life After Jillian

I think grief is something like raking leaves. After you get them all raked up and are feeling a tad better, the wind blows them out into the yard again. It seems like you do the same work over and over, but I think there are less leaves after a while.

David Barr

Within weeks of Jillian's death, I was shocked to see how quickly we reverted to thinking about ourselves. Without Jillian in our midst to keep us focused on what was important in life, we quickly forgot. But we did not forget completely. Jillian left a permanent mark on us: a draw toward people with special needs or people experiencing loss and grief.

Luke had started his Eagle Project (a final service project to complete the requirements for becoming an Eagle Scout) at Harris Hillman weeks before Jillian died. The school had not had a yearbook for 15 years. Luke, as a ninth grader, had a semester of journalism class under his belt. He met with the principal, Robbie Hampton, and asked if he could make a yearbook for the school as his Eagle Scout project. The principal's enthusiastic response fueled Luke, and he researched computer programs, timelines, and costs. Soon a plan was in place. Luke announced the project at a morning staff meeting, and we were off. When Jillian died suddenly two weeks later, we asked, "Should he continue?" Luke wanted to proceed, and the next months following her death he spent documenting her school, her teachers, and her friends. I helped as his liaison, getting photos he needed or quotes from teachers during the school day. It was an amazing place to grieve and work through our pain in loosing Jillian as we interacted with other children struggling to breathe or walk or communicate. Despite their disadvantages, these students were happy and full of life. We especially loved the title pages for the different sections of the yearbook. The art teacher at the time was one of the first to get a digital camera. She took many close-up pictures of students in all the classes, maybe ten or twenty in a row of one child. Because children with handicaps cannot smile on cue, she chose to take candid photos and was able to catch students at their best. Some were laughing, some just looking intently, some holding hands with a caregiver. We used these pictures to make collages for the title pages, and they captured the essence of the school. The books came out in May, four months after Jillian died. We were grateful Jillian had experienced this community for the last season of her life.

After Jillian's funeral, Paul and I began to find new homes for her equipment, adapted toys, and even our conversion van with the lift. He knew a family that had a son and daughter with special needs. They could use our therapy table and other equipment, and they purchased our van. Other items, like her wheelchair and shower chair, we donated to United Cerebral Palsy. They have a room filled with used equipment, where caregivers can get items to use with their children for free. We had found a used car seat and a soft chair for Jillian there years earlier. Knowing Jillian's belongings would serve other children helped our grief. Rachel wanted to move into Jillian's room, so we let her. Somehow being in Jillian's space nurtured Rachel, and we did not redecorate or remove all of Jillian from the room. Instead, Rachel lived with her things and talked about Jillian for months. Even years later, Rachel might wear socks or use a headband that had belonged to Jillian and she always remembered the connection.

One year after her death, we went to the gravesite as a family. The thirty-minute drive out into the countryside gave us time to share memories and stories about Jillian. It was the first time we had all been back to the gravesite together. Later at home we watched a video of her funeral—again a first time for us all. We wrote down our reflections on the day and year. I include them because we wrote them as they happened, not years later.

Since Rachel could not write, she drew a picture. She called it "Tears—Because Jillian misses us."

Andrew (now in 8th grade) wrote a poem:

The pain of age
As the days go by
Getting worse and worse
Until the day she will die

But it brought us together
Making us one
Even without her
Life can be fun

Let us remember her fun
Let us remember her smile
And just try to remember
We'll see her in awhile

Luke, a high school sophomore, wrote:

> I can't believe it has only been 1 year. It seems like forever. Our lives have changed so much. New cars, new rooms. I could remember vividly the lift process [getting her in and out of the van] when I saw the video. I always think it is strange to see video of someone who is dead because for a few moments, they are alive again. I'll always remember how nice her hair was.

Paul wrote:

> After taking time to visit Jillian's grave and watching her funeral today, I miss some specific aspects of her presence.
>
> I miss her grounding force in our family. Jillian brought out the best in all of us. We will have to seek out and work to serve "the least of these" from now on.
>
> I miss the sweet familiarity of lifting, turning, changing, and caring for her everyday needs. I loved pushing her through new places and routine routes.
>
> Jillian's funeral time, and that week in general, represents the most powerful outpouring of God's Spirit that I have ever experienced. The energy I experienced reminded me of riding a huge wave. I know it was situational, but I still long to carry that anointing through life and care for my family at that level all the time.

I wrote:

> Jillian, I like seeing who you were in our family a few

> years ago. You look beautiful and soft and graceful. Our family is laughing and you are hanging out. Rachel is so cute running around and the boys are boys, not young men like they are now. You would be impressed with how strong they both are. Rachel could push you all by herself now and do the tie-downs [for the wheelchair in the van].
>
> The memorial garden is an empty place. You are not there. But the weathered wind chime makes me smile.
>
> The empty wheelchair in the receiving line was the most emotional thing. Because it is your chair—so much a part of you—and yet so empty.
>
> Really everything is empty. You are not here. Your box of stuff is like fall leaves collected in their beauty and now crumpled and dry and brown. But it is not a sad empty. It is just reality.
>
> Our relationship is on hold until we are together again.

Heaven certainly seemed more real to all of us. Now we knew she would be there to greet us. Ever since that first-year anniversary, I have marked her birthday, not her death, in the life of our family. Every November 19th I still make her birthday meal of potato soup and cheesecake—two things she could taste by mouth over the years. Sometimes I walk with one of her caregivers at the lake nearby. On the anniversary of her death, I usually take a retreat day and read or walk; one of the first years, I painted with watercolors at her gravesite.

Luke, Andrew, and Rachel carry Jillian's impact with them. Luke finished the Harris Hillman yearbook in the months after Jillian died. Two years later, he wrote his college application essay about the two people who influenced him the most in his life. One was Jillian, and the other was his dad. This is his paragraph about Jillian:

> My sister was a joyful girl with beautiful red hair. She also had Rett syndrome, a genetic condition that left her completely disabled. She could not speak, but her actions spoke volumes to the people around her. She was the ultimate lesson in contentment. I remember that I would look at her and see that she had nothing. She could not run with the other children her age. She even had difficulty turning her head to look at someone. However, she was constantly smiling. This girl, who occupied a broken body, was content despite all of her horrible circumstances. It was amazing just to watch her laugh at the tinkling of a wind chime. She taught me so much by her beautiful example, and I learned patience and peacefulness from her silent existence. I also grew to be comfortable around people with special needs. I think that my family is as strong as it is today because of her presence. When Jillian died two years ago at age eleven, an astonishing number of people attended her funeral. I was so happy to see that she had reached into the hearts of so many, all without saying a word.

In college, Luke volunteered with a local buddy program for kids with autism and other disabilities. He became good friends with his assigned "buddy." Several weekends he babysat for his buddy and siblings, comfortable with the family dynamic.

Andrew worked three summers in high school at summer programs for children with special needs. Here is his college application essay, based on his experiences with Jillian and those he got to know in the four years after she died.

> On a strikingly hot day in July, a small older neighborhood is struck with a strange scene. Three grown children, being pushed in wheelchairs, roll by while three others follow, holding hands with supervising adults. This is Camp Possible for special needs children going on their daily walk around the neighborhood. As the midday sun beats down upon the walkers, one of the girls begins to twitch and then violently shake. She is having a seizure, and as her eyes close some of the helpers begin to panic. They are about a block and a half from their air-conditioned building, and no one can carry the girl that far. This is where I come in. As one of the volunteer counselors at the camp, I played with the children and often went on these routine walks. I propose that I try to carry the 90-pound girl back to the camp center. They agree to let me try, and I carry the girl in my arms back while she continues to seize. She recovers in the cool air and is later sent to the hospital.
>
> My work at this camp was inspired by my sister, Jillian, who was only two years younger than me. At about one year of age, Jillian began to regress in her development and was diagnosed with Rett syndrome. This meant she could never walk or talk, and she had to be fed though a feeding tube. Although this was a devastating blow to our family, Jillian turned out to be a blessing in disguise. When others are weak, it brings out the best in those around them because the one who is

weak needs so much help. Jillian literally brought out the best in all of us. She exemplified patience, as she sat through endless activities she could not partake in, and as she lay quiet in bed in the morning, unable to rise and begin the day. Jillian brought out the caring servant in me. If she needed to be strapped into the car, I would be there to do it. If she needed to be pushed around in a dance with music playing, I would gladly be her dance partner.

She brought our family together to a place of unity. There was no reason to bicker and fight when we saw what she had to go through each and every day. She gave us a unique perspective on life that most families have not had the privilege of experiencing. Unfortunately, her body became increasingly challenged so that she choked frequently and cried late at night. She died suddenly after a brief illness when I was in seventh grade, and she was in fifth, and I don't feel my family or I have been the same since. When we sat around the dinner table a week after her death, I was quoted as saying, "I think we got along better when Jillian was alive." Of course the previous week had been an exception, but that statement rings true today. She drew us together in a special way, and although she remains in memory, the sense of selflessness she promoted is somewhat dimmed.

If it weren't for Jillian, I would have never worked at the several special needs camps I have attended over the years. She showed me how to be compassionate and patient with these children. The truth is, it is probably more fun and rewarding to spend the day with a special

> needs child than hanging out with my normal friends. A mentally disabled child has no hidden agenda, or personal greed. They love you just for playing with them or helping them eat. Jillian helped me understand life is not always about my enjoyment. Bringing these kids joy was more important than playing basketball with my friends. It was more fun to play basketball with my new friend with Down's syndrome anyway. He didn't care if he or I won. He cared that I loved him and wanted to be with him, and thanks to Jillian and my new understanding of life, that was the only place I wanted to be.

After completing his freshman year at college, Andrew took a year off and worked at Jillian's school, Harris Hillman, as a special education assistant. The students in his classroom were Jillian's peers, nearly eighteen-years-old. One girl had been in a group therapy class with Jillian as a baby, and now this young woman enjoyed being with Andrew. Since Andrew was in seventh grade when Jillian died, he had not been big enough for most caregiving. As an adult caring for his sister's peers, he could identify with Jillian in a deeper place.

Rachel does not remember many details about Jillian, but she feels at home with children and adults with special needs. After Jillian died, Rachel would announce suddenly to our waitress at a restaurant or the extra-happy salesperson at the Disney Store, "my sister died." That is a conversation killer, but it gave us opportunity to fill in the blanks for strangers, and it helped in the healing process. Having a young child in the house unafraid to talk about an uncomfortable subject brought our memories to the surface and kept Jillian front and center. Several summers, Rachel has volunteered with me at Harris Hillman. Also, when she was in fifth grade, we had the opportunity to go to Kyrgyzstan on a medical teaching trip. Rachel, Paul, and I visited several groups of kids with special needs and helped with medical and equipment needs. Rachel gets down on the floor with special kids here or across the world, completely at home.

The hardest part now about not having Jillian in the family is that ten years have gone by, and we have new friends and acquaintances that did not know us as a family with Jillian. They do not even see the empty space. They do not know her story or mine. It is a challenging subject to bring up in casual conversations, and every time someone asks me how many children I have, I face a decision. I am comfortable talking about Jillian, but to people who do not know, it is a shock to hear that I had a child with multiple special needs, took care of her for 11 years, and then lost her. I have learned when to talk about it, and sometimes telling Jillian's story afresh brings me great joy. Whether or not others perceive it, Jillian's role in our family—both in her living and in her dying—constitutes a large part of our family DNA.

I still volunteer at Jillian's school. I never made the decision to participate because I want to serve others or do something good. I simply have a continual draw to walk those halls, see the kids, and speak with the staff. Here is an article I wrote for the school newsletter, read by other caretaking parents and the special education staff, in February 2006:

One Year Out: Reflections on Losing a Child

> We lost our eleven-year-old daughter, Jillian, a year ago. She had a viral infection, and suddenly her heart developed an arrhythmia that the doctors could not fix.

While her death was sudden and unexpected, she was at risk for premature death because of her disabilities.

Jillian has two older brothers, now 15 and 14, and a younger sister, age 6. I would like to share with you a few aspects of our journey this past year.

Most people feel the loss of a child is catastrophic. And it is. But we lost a lot of our daughter years ago when she regressed in her development as a baby. There were so many losses along the way as she missed milestones, lost what ground she had, and suffered the distorting of her body. We tried as a family to look those losses in the face and grieve them, while at the same time receiving who she was and the gift that she was. This year has been a continuation in that path of simultaneous grieving and rejoicing that began with her diagnosis.

As you all know, caring for a disabled person is challenging: anticipating needs for someone who cannot tell you, managing the medical treatments for a complicated patient, balancing the needs of this child with the rest of your family and your own life. These are hard things. We have seen since Jillian is gone, how she called us to a place of unselfishness that was good for us as individuals and as a family. Having someone around you who constantly demands that you think outside of yourself is truly a gift. After Jillian died, my then-thirteen-year-old son said, “Mom, I don’t think we get along as well as we did when Jillian was with us.” And he was right. Jillian called us to a higher place.

We recently took our first big family vacation without Jillian. We flew to Southern California for a family

> reunion. I don't know about you, but when we traveled with Jillian, we had to really function well as a family just to survive! My husband and I had to work as a team. The boys had to help push the wheelchair or corral their younger sister. Everyone had a job. Now it is easier. The boys can listen to their music, Paul can nap, I can read, but we are at risk for being short with each other, self-absorbed and independent. This time, we had to fight to be a team, even though the trip was so much easier. We are not Jillian's ambassadors anymore. We are just a regular family. It is not bad to be a regular family, but I missed what Jillian called out in others as we pushed her chair. She brought out the best in people, in us, and in those we met.
>
> I miss Jillian's smell. I miss her soft hands, her furtive glances, her smile given when least expected. I miss her simply being present.
>
> She taught me that suffering is wretched and that wretchedness must be faced. But even when we want to run away so bad, brokenness brings a kind of life on this earth nothing else can. I don't know how you feel about heaven, but one day my body and mind will be broken, too. And I think she will be waiting to greet me. I'm excited about that day.
>
> The work that you do, the caregiving you offer, the tears you shed, the love and joy you give and receive on your journey with these children, is some of the most important and transforming work on the planet.

So I keep coming back to her school. I like being able to push wheelchairs on a field trip or take pictures of students for the newsletter. I like being on campus where people know my journey. Also, when I meet someone with a child with special needs, I bring them to her school. A few years after Jillian's death, we even had the opportunity to get our friends involved in a memorial project.

Many people donated money in honor of Jillian's life to either Vanderbilt Children's Hospital or Harris Hillman School. The hospital donations went to the construction of the new children's hospital. Jillian's name is engraved on a butterfly in the Butterfly Garden, a commemorative display of colorful spinning butterflies in the lobby of the new hospital. The money donated to Harris Hillman remained in a fund for over two years until a suitable project came up. When the school was remodeled in the fall of 2007, a plan for an outdoor sensory garden emerged. The Metro School system created the fenced garden with a shade portico, three fountains, and outdoor activity centers. Classrooms added wind chimes, bright flowers, and a student designed mosaic. Jillian's memorial fund paid for a musician/instrument fabricator to do an instrument-building workshop at the school. Over 50 volunteers came together during the three-day period and constructed a large, accessible, free-standing marimba and three tongue drums out of all-weather materials. When Jillian was alive, she loved to go to the children's museum in Chattanooga, where she could play various instruments. We have a picture of her and her grandma playing a marimba made by this

same fabricator about fifteen years ago. I think she would be delighted with this garden and the instruments. Paul and I enjoyed hosting the fabricator, helping with the project, and continuing to celebrate Jillian's life. Just last summer when Rachel and I volunteered at the Harris Hillman summer school, we took children out to this garden and helped them play the marimba and drums.

I have several friends who are moms to kids with special needs. We have a unique bond. I have found myself over the years telling the same stories over and over to these moms of the things I learned from Jillian. I remember that, after we got Jillian's diagnosis, I tried to get any book that related to what I was going through, and it seemed few existed. One friend I had when Jillian was about five is Nancy Guthrie. She has written about her experiences having two children with a universally fatal genetic illness. Both died as babies, and she has chronicled her journey, questions, and revelations. At the funeral for her daughter Hope, Nancy's husband David talked about how, as parents, we raise our children for the future—when they will sleep through the night, when they will walk, when they will go to school, when they will go to college. He said that he and Nancy had learned the importance of raising and enjoying their children for the present—for the moment—as that is all they had. David encouraged us not to let the future rob us of the present. Parents like the Guthries helped me gain perspective on my journey with Jillian and with my other kids, perspectives that are as real to me today as they were in the crucible of our lives with Jillian.

I also have a friend named Owen. On a hot summer day last year, my daughter Rachel and I drove to his home in the Tennessee countryside. His family had just installed a pool, and we were invited to swim with Owen and his mother. In the clear water, Owen laughed, kicked, and watched my daughter swim under him blowing bubbles. Later, his blonde hair swooshed out of his tan face, he enjoyed watermelon; like any child, he ate until pink juice ran down his chin. Owen has cerebral palsy. At seven years of age, he is dependent on his parents for moving, eating, and learning. I like holding Owen on my lap, whispering in his ear, and seeing his shy smile or hearing his belly laugh. I like supporting him in the water, and feeling him enjoy the weightlessness and freedom of movement.

I grieve that Owen cannot run and play in his skateboarder shoes or jump in the pool and make waves with my daughter. My heart aches when he has to go to the hospital, have another surgery, or endure seizures. I watch his parents walk the tension of meeting his physical needs and still pursuing a fun and meaningful life as a family. But in all the complexity of equipment and medicines and therapies, Owen shines. Jesus said, "Blessed are the pure in heart, for they will see God" (Matthew 5:8 NIV). Why do the pure in heart see God? Is it because they are not distracted by tasks, worry, and competition? People like Owen—like Jillian—remind us of what is truly important, what it means to be a person, what is real.

The New Testament writers talk about suffering and the fruit it yields. They compare the suffering of the early church with the agony Jesus endured by taking on our humanity and dying on the cross. Paul says, "I want to know Christ and the power of his resurrection and the fellowship of sharing in his sufferings" (Philippians 3:10 NIV). Peter admonishes, "So then, those who suffer according to God's will should commit themselves to their faithful Creator and continue to do good" (1Peter 4:19 NIV). James declares, "Consider it pure joy, my brothers, whenever you face trials of many kinds" (James 1:2 NIV). They are calling the early church to embrace their suffering, as Jesus embraced his. He walked in unmatched fellowship with God, sinless, healing others, yet he suffered much. And Jesus, like the writers of the New Testament, experienced God's provision and intimacy in the center of his anguish.

As Owen's mother says, "This is my path. This is what I know." She pushes the wheelchair and lets Owen do his transforming work on those who have eyes to see and ears to hear.

Those who sow in tears will reap with songs of joy.
He who goes out weeping, carrying seed to sow,
will return with songs of joy, carrying sheaves with him.
Psalm 126:5-6 NIV

Conclusion

Christianity…ultimately offers no theoretical solution at all. It merely points to the cross and says that, practically speaking, there is no evil so dark and so obscene—not even this—but that God can turn it to good.

Frederick Beuchner

Even in darkness light dawns for the upright. *Psalm 112:4 NIV*

Dear Jillian,

I have just finished writing a book about your life, our journey together, and what we learned from that journey. I don't know how to end the story. It seems incomplete, yet I have no new information, no poignant stories, no more revelations found while walking out our life together. I often wonder what other stories I would have had, were you still alive today. I wonder about the positive impact you could have had with more years, but also the pain those years would have cost you. I am older now. I need reading glasses and I fatigue quickly; I wonder if I would have been up to the task and could have been flexible enough—strong enough—to keep caring for you. On the most visceral level, I would do anything to once again bury my nose in your neck, hold your soft hand or brush out your beautiful hair. The acuteness of how miserable you were in your body those last months has faded from my memory. While I know it is true, I do not feel it anymore, and so I want you back.

The students whose class you joined at Christ Presbyterian Academy are now seniors, thinking about college, getting ready for prom, turning their eyes toward adulthood. I wonder if they remember you. Will they say to their spouse one day, or their child "When I was in kindergarten there was this girl…"? Yesterday as I drove to pick up Rachel, one boy from your kindergarten class turned at the intersection in front of my waiting car. Our eyes locked for a moment. Does he remember me like I remember him and how he was around you?

Aside from your gentle presence, the thing I miss most is how black-and-white you made our daily lives. There was no room for moping around or entertaining frivolities in our heads. Your existence demanded realness of perspective and action. I spoke recently with a friend diagnosed with cancer about how sharpening suffering and loss are to our daily perspective. Suddenly, what really is important in life—the things authors have touted through the ages—is obvious. Of course, one potential outcome of suffering is bitterness, loss of hope, and destitution. But those who press into suffering and let God do His transforming work experience rare treasure.

In the years following your diagnosis and death, I have considered myself a card-carrying sufferer, meaning that I have the experience to interact significantly with others who are suffering. Paul writes in 2 Corinthians 1:3-5 NIV:

> "Praise be to the God and Father of our Lord Jesus Christ, the Father of compassion and the God of all comfort, who comforts us in all our troubles, so that we can comfort those in any trouble with the comfort we ourselves receive from God. For just as we share abundantly in the sufferings of Christ, so also our comfort abounds through Christ."

People seem to find comfort in knowing I too have touched deep suffering. I can stand in that place of utter devastation with them and not feel the need to say something or fix it. Those who know my story also know the fruit and know that God did not abandon them, me, or our family in our distress. We can say that 1 Peter 5:10 is true: "And the God of all grace, who called you to his eternal glory in Christ, after you have suffered a little while, will himself restore you and make you strong, firm and steadfast." I have friends who have lost their husbands or children, lived through unemployment, or coped with devastating medical news. I try to communicate to them—with or without words—the dual lesson distilled from our experience together; loss is excruciatingly painful, and God will turn evil into good.

I never feel like you are still with me. I do not sense your presence near me or feel any "life" associated with you. I feel like you are away on a trip and I will see you again someday. What stories will you tell me? Andrew heard about near-death stories in high school: the good encounters people have with relatives who have died, warm sensations and bright light, and conversations with supernatural beings. He also heard about the bad encounters full of negative images that frighten people into changing their lives when they are brought back to life. Andrew's take-home message from hearing this was that an afterlife must be real—there are so many similarities of stories from around the world. He was so excited because he really believed now that he would see you again.

When you were alive, I told a group of women that you were my role model. You were so peaceful with yourself: so free from blaming yourself, blaming others, or blaming your bad luck. You received every day and what unfolded with grace and acceptance. You had been forced to die to yourself when you regressed, and now, trapped in a ruined body, you were free simply to live and enjoy what you could. I am not there yet, but I know it is possible.

I love you, precious girl, gift from God, gentle daughter. With the perspective of eternity I can say, "See you soon!"

Love, Mom

Afterword

The View From Four of Jillian's Caregivers

So Joshua fought the Amalekites as Moses had ordered, and Moses, Aaron and Hur went to the top of the hill. As long as Moses held up his hands, the Israelites were winning, but whenever he lowered his hands, the Amalekites were winning. When Moses' hands grew tired, they took a stone and put it under him and he sat on it. Aaron and Hur held his hands up—one on one side, one on the other—so that his hands remained steady till sunset.

Exodus 17:10-12 NIV

Over the years, many people supported us and aided us as we took care of Jillian. Some came up to me and said, "How is Jillian? I have been praying for her this morning". Others opened the door for her wheelchair. Some saved her an aisle seat in church or spoke to her directly, acknowledging that she was a real child. God also raised up several women to work more intimately with Jillian. I presented what Jennifer Martin said about her relationship with Jillian from her eulogy, but I want to give voice to the others who knew my daughter almost as well as I did. These women were her friends first and my friends second. They held me up the way Aaron and Hur held Moses.

KRISTINA

Kristina Quiram worked with Jillian one or two half-days a week from the time Jillian was 18 months old until she started kindergarten,. She also babysat all our kids many times throughout Jillian's life, went on several family vacations with us, and took care of Jillian when I was out of town. Kristina was 15 when she started working with us. Being homeschooled, she had a flexible schedule. She loved children and worked in our church nursery. At first, she stayed with Jillian at our home while I was present doing housework or taking care of the boys. As time went on Kristina came to know Jillian and our family so well, she took on greater responsibility. She went to California twice with us, to Pittsburgh to see my family, and to Chattanooga for a long weekend. Far from detracting from our family time, she became part of our family and someone the boys remember fondly from their childhood.

Kristina recalls working with Jillian during her regression:

> I remember she was still able to sit in her high chair when I first started and then continued to lose trunk control. She had good eye contact in the beginning and that lessened as time went on. She could purposefully smile the entire time I knew her.

She did everything with Jillian:

> I played with Jill—sat on the floor with her and helped her use her hands to manipulate toys, helped her create art at the table in her chair, took her for walks, swung her in the hammock, gave her showers, sang to her, fed her (food in the beginning and then feeding tube later), read to her, painted her toenails, danced with her. I went on outings to help with her sometimes and also went with her to preschool to be her helper there. Later on I did her exercises with her that the physical therapist had given her to do—moving her legs and stretching, etc.

I asked Kristina what she learned from working with Jillian, and she had three responses:

> First, one thing that I learned is that a family with a special needs child can live "normally." And what I mean by that is that you all didn't let it limit your life as a family. You took trips and she came along; you lived life as you otherwise would have (it seemed) and helped her participate as much as she was able. You didn't try to hide her or hibernate away from the world. I think that

> before I knew you guys, I thought that having a special needs child would end your chance to live life fully, but you all participated in community life, service, and travel as much or even more so than most families do. A real inspiration.
>
> Second, I would never have believed or imagined it possible to develop a meaningful connection with someone like Jillian. How do you connect with someone who is so limited in his or her communication? But I learned that the more time and energy I gave her—the more I learned to read her and interpret her mood—the more I felt I knew and understood her. Were there worlds inside of her I didn't know? Of course, but being able to receive what little she could offer—a smile, an intentional look in my direction—was a treasure that I will forever hold dear.
>
> Third, God used knowing Jillian to teach me about Kingdom values. As a Christian, I believe that God loves me based not on anything I do, but simply because I am His child. The thing is, I believe this in theory, but often live like my striving will gain me good standing with God. Developing a love for someone who can't actively show his or her love back helped me to understand the heart of God towards me. I loved her for who she was and not because of anything she could do. Those with special needs remind us of the sacredness of life alone.

The pivotal moment of Jillian's funeral was when Kristina performed a dance she had choreographed to Chris Rice's

"Untitled Hymn." Kristina, then age 24, trained as a classical ballerina throughout her youth. At the time of Jillian's death, she was not actively dancing but pulled on all she knew to create a gift for us and for Jillian. This is what she shared about the process:

> How can someone dance at a funeral? As a Christian, I believe we are all held bondage to decay while we are in this world. None of us is whole. Though we may feel on top of the world, we are only limping along when compared to what we were made for—perfection, holiness, union with God. And yet when others who are not outwardly broken such as Jillian have died, there is nothing but grief. While her death was a painful loss and made me struggle with the fact that God chose not to heal her, it was a thing to celebrate as well—just as every crossing over should be. In preparing for and then dancing at her funeral, I realized that the lips that had never said a word or sung a note were filled with accolades to the King—in His very presence! The feet and legs that never took a step were twirling and leaping free of their chains! It was a powerful moment for me to both grieve and rejoice—such is the mysterious nature of this journey in Christ.

Kristina is now married and has three small children of her own. Her Christmas family photo smiles at me on our fridge. Kristina is one of the many gifts Jillian brought into my life and the life of my family.

Mary Britton

Mary Britton Cummings worked two to three mornings a week for over a year when Jillian was three. I had been a guest speaker at Mary Britton's undergraduate special education class:

> I was a junior at Vanderbilt, and you came to speak to my class about how families relate to professionals working with their children with special needs. At the end of the class, you said that you were looking for some help in the summer with Jillian and passed around a sign up sheet for anyone interested. I am so glad that our paths crossed then!

Mary Britton stopped working with Jillian to do her student teaching but continued over the years to babysit Jillian or all three children occasionally, even staying overnight. We all went to her wedding when Jillian was seven. Mary Britton recalls how she spent time with Jillian:

> Jillian and I would do a lot of sensory things together. We would play with Play-Doh and talk about how it felt. We spent a lot of time outside on walks talking about the sounds, and she loved to be on the hammock with her brothers. We did some communication work where I would give her choices and ask her to make a choice with her eyes. Because she loved music so much, we also would listen to music and dance along to the beat. I remember reading lots of books with her, getting her to touch things that were in the book if there were some

> textures. I loved when Luke and Andrew were home because we would all play games together like hide and seek, or we would build towers with the boys' Legos. I was Jillian's assistant at Judson Baptist one summer for one or two mornings a week.

Like Kristina, Mary Britton intersected with Jillian at the end of her regression. She was also present when we discovered Jillian was having seizures. As a special education student, she brought practical skills from her classes to use with Jillian:

> I remember that we thought she was learning to smile when she was responding to books, music, etc. You then found out that she was having seizures when she was smiling and laughing often. She was started on a medicine that I remember made her very sleepy. I do remember her being fussy, especially when I would babysit at night. I would use music and the walks outside to help her calm down. I also remember that she liked the beads in her room doorway and that when she was fussy, we would play in her room with music on and lights off. There were other sensory activities that seemed to calm her down when she was fussy.

Mary Britton recalls one day shortly after Jillian developed seizures:

> You came home and said how the traffic was so bad and how it was making you frustrated and late. As you were sitting in traffic you said you thought about how Jillian has so many seizures daily and how she tolerated them

> so beautifully. You said, "If Jillian can have all these seizures without much complaint, then I can handle the traffic without complaint as well." I have shared this story with others as a way that Jillian was a great teacher of many spiritual lessons.

Mary Britton saw how Jillian's brokenness called out the best in our boys:

> I also remember feeling this same way about Luke and Andrew. They loved and gave so much to Jillian without her being able to give much in return to two young boys. Since the boys were young, I think they got the spiritual teachings that Jillian had to offer more easily than adults do. They understood her patience, gentleness, and her unconditional love. I have told many people that when I was in your home, I always felt that there was so much love and kindness between your children. Of course Luke and Andrew were naturally kind children, but I do think that Jillian really taught them about what is important to value in life. They learned these lessons at a very young age, and it was always so apparent to me when I spent time with them.

Mary Britton taught in several different special education settings before starting a family. She has a unique perspective as an educator and former caregiver on the value of children with special needs in our communities:

> I think children are our best spiritual teachers. They are able to be present and honest and forgiving without

meditating or doing yoga or going on long weekend retreats. Children with special needs to me are even greater teachers of religion and living out the lessons that Jesus was sent to earth to teach.

Like many spiritual teachings, this one for me does present conflict. After giving birth to four healthy children, I feel that there is no greater blessing than a healthy child. I am certain as well that there is no greater heartbreak than watching a child struggle with disability or illness. However, in my professional experience and in my personal relationships with families who have children with special needs, I have heard again and again that through this heartbreak, families feel closer to God and thankful for the lessons that their children with disabilities teach them. While I don't know any parent that hopes for a child to have special needs, I do think it is impossible for one's life not to be enriched by the lessons that children with special needs teach us. The lessons that I have learned from children with special needs are to love unconditionally, to live without judging others, and that the simple pleasures in life are really the most sacred. Watching a child smile while being pushed on a hammock with her brothers is more valuable than any degree or material possession. When I feel myself getting caught up in trivial life matters, I remind myself to look to my children and to the lessons that other children have taught me through the years. Jillian taught me so much about music, love, and patience, and I am so thankful for my time with sweet Jillian.

CHRISTINE

I visited Christine Smith at her home to gather her reflections on her time with Jillian. Our time was punctuated by her two grandsons' arrival for the afternoon. As she held one and took care of the other, it reminded me of her season in our home.

Christine began cleaning my home when Jillian was almost three. In fact, the first gathering we got ready for together was Jillian's third birthday party. There would be many more in our future together. A mutual friend had given me Christine's name, and I called her to see if she had a day to clean my house. She did not, but said things might change and I should call back in a few weeks. Over the next few months, I called and we would chat; she still had no free day. I looked for help elsewhere but nothing happened, and she would always say she would like to help me out and maybe something would open up. And then it did! Christine remembers, "When I first came, Jillian was small enough that I could pick her up and put her in my arms and rock her." Christine cleaned my house and helped with laundry. With three small children and therapy appointments, this was invaluable. During that time, Christine was often around Jillian:

> I was getting to know Jillian, getting used to what her needs were. I would get in her face, play with her hair, and talk to her. I spent bits of time with her, and we developed a relationship. I learned her way to communicate, what she meant by her hand and body movements, the shift of her eyes. There was life there and it was real and tangible, something you could touch in her.

Christine began accompanying Jillian to a regular preschool, where she did hand-over-hand art work with Jillian and helped her interact with the other kids: "I liked seeing her joy at accomplishment and the joy she had in the other kids—the sparkle in her eye—she knew they were kids like her."

Christine continues: "When I started feeding her, that was a real treat. That was a whole other level of communication. There is always a fellowship in food!" Over the nine years Christine worked with Jillian, she performed many roles. When we homeschooled Jillian, Christine laid out the activities for the day on a table—maybe painting and toys and stories. She talked to Jillian about all the options and then let Jillian decide what they would do first. "I could tell what she wanted by how she looked," Christine says. This choice-making is called "eye gaze" in special education, and Christine discovered that Jillian said much with and through her eyes:

> She loved to be read to and I would show her the pictures. We would take walks, talking about the trees; she liked being in the sun—not bright sun, but springtime sun. Sometimes I would run with her in her chair. She liked to go fast! I would roll her over the grass to the creek and bring over some water for her to touch. One of the things I enjoyed was dancing with her. She would laugh out loud. I would turn the music up loud, and we would dance before the Lord. I told her the angels were dancing with us. I know she understood. Her spirit would come alive.

Later, Christine incorporated Rachel into time with Jillian: "I would put Rachel, when she was a baby, in Jillian's arms. In time they could both play on the same level and do it together. We did Play-Doh, dressed dolls, played house—you know, kid play!" Christine also helped give Jillian showers, combed her hair, and picked out clothes for her to wear:

> I would put bows or barrettes in her hair. Sometimes I would French braid her hair and let her watch me in the mirror. Jillian was an overcomer. She was happy even with all the pains she had. The therapy I did with her—I am sure that was uncomfortable sometimes, but she always came back with a smile. She was happy to see me. I always felt accepted and loved.

She recalls the day Jillian died:

> I lost a dear friend. I lost someone real close to me, like a grandchild. I knew her from such a young age. She was like a child to me. She grew bigger, but her innocence was still a child's. She was sweet, gentle, had genuine trust and faith. Her death was a real loss to me. She was locked inside physically but not spiritually. It was good knowing she was going to heaven. I wanted to honor Jillian and celebrate her life in Jesus and her victory in him. There was a lot to her. I couldn't sum her up in a few words. But at the same time she was not trapped anymore—it was bittersweet.

Jillian died so quickly and unexpectedly, I was grateful I could reach almost all her caregivers by phone. Christine remembers the call:

> I came to the hospital, and Stephen, my husband, went with me. I was so glad you called and that I had the opportunity to let her go, to give myself permission—to give her permission to go. It helped me be at peace with letting her go. At the same time, it was sorrowful. She looked peaceful—she knew she would be with the Lord.

Christine continued to work in my home for eight months after Jillian died. Now she spent more time with Rachel: driving her to preschool, going out to get icees, sitting together in the treehouse: "Rachel and I talked about Jillian. Her things, which we still played with, reminded me of her. There was an empty spot. Our normal thing had changed. Something was missing in the household." Christine's relationship with Rachel during those months helped Rachel process the loss of her sister. I had the gift of grieving with Christine, someone who loved Jillian and my family so much. As the end of August approached and with it the start of kindergarten for Rachel, my need for help ended, and Christine retired.

Today, Christine reflects on Jillian's impact on her life:

> Now I see her smiling! I see her peace and her love for the Lord. She never held any ill feeling. She would make other people happy and could put people at ease. It's like she was saying, "I'm in this chair, but it's OK!" That's the message she communicated.

JANE

I spent an afternoon with Jane Carroll, one of Jillian's caregivers and friends. We began our time reflecting on the central question, "What makes someone valuable?" When questions like this have come up over the many years since her death, Jane thinks of Jillian: "We are precious, hands down. Jillian couldn't produce anything concrete, yet all the intangibles she had in spades." Jane saw Jillian impact people time and again as they got past her brokenness and saw her joy in life. After watching Jillian journey through her second regression, she saw Jillian's crying give way to peace. Her value in God's eyes because of who she was "became the deep truth she carried."

Jane's relationship with Jillian began when Jillian was just over a year old. Jane held Jillian while she homeschooled her children one day a week. This gave me a break, but I always felt Jane did it primarily because she enjoyed Jillian. Jane says of that time:

> Jillian was such a blessing to us. She brought out the best in all of us. My kids would want to show what they were working on to Jillian, a kind of competition! Jillian affected people in two ways: first she helped set their head straight. The fact that other people had it harder than they did, that my problems aren't so bad. But that was just the outer edge of knowing Jillian. After you were around her, you saw she enjoyed nature and was content simply being alive. My kids sensed she might have preferences and they thought making her happy

was a worthy goal. They were well rewarded if she smiled because they knew it wasn't insincere.

As Jane's children got older and Jillian started preschool, Jane did not take care of Jillian except on the odd occasion when I needed a sitter. When Jillian started kindergarten at her brothers' private Christian school, she needed an assistant to go with her. This assistant would help Jillian access what was happening at school and would act as her translator for the staff and kids. Jane went two mornings a week for almost two school years until Jillian got too fussy to stay in her chair so long. Jane remembers, "I enjoyed helping the kids love her. Some kids got her right away." That year, several of the students were dealing with hard life issues. One had recently lost her father to a sudden heart attack. One had an older brother who was dying of an aggressive cancer. One had a mother who was battling cancer. Having Jillian in her brokenness sitting in the classroom seemed to help. Jane brought up Jillian's birthday that fall. I came in as a surprise while the students, including Jillian and Jane, were at P.E. and decorated each chair with a helium balloon. I put frosted sugar cookies and drinks on each desk. When the children arrived back from P.E., everyone was so excited to see the room! Jillian was happy, beaming. Jane says, "She was one of them. They loved each other. They were a group."

Jillian stayed at home for the conclusion of her first grade year and for second and third grade. During those two years, Jane came to my home two days a week and helped me and other caregivers homeschool Jillian. This schedule allowed us to flow with Jillian's routine, and we were able to maximize times she felt good. Jane says of those days:

> I loved walking around the garden with her and looking at the different flowers. I noticed things more in showing them to her: planes, clouds, flowers, textures, smells. There were smaller movements, touching hands. I loved reading chapter books to her, lying on our backs. There was a sense of fellowship. I also enjoyed incorporating Rachel into my time with Jillian—playing American Girl dolls, the three of us, or pushing Jillian with Rachel riding on her lap. Of course I liked to dance with her and twirl her. One time you took us to the mall, and you were there with your mother-in-law. You gave me some money to shop with Jillian. We went into a store and bought a feather boa. When I rolled her out with that boa on to show you both, she was beaming!

Jane's father came to live with her during the time she worked in my home. He was 85 and suffering from severe dementia. Jane often brought her father to my home and he sat in my bright living room and let my household go on around him. Sometimes he would read to preschooler Rachel when she brought him a book. It was special season. One day, the three ladies that cleaned my house during those years came to clean while a care coordinator with the state was visiting us. So Jane, her father, the cleaning ladies, and the care coordinator were all in my home because of my child. What an interesting community, brought together through Jillian's brokenness! Jane talked about her father's relationship with Jillian: "He had no trouble enjoying Jillian. It all made sense to him. He enjoyed having her sit nearby, appreciating her presence. Later, when he couldn't talk, he was still glad to come and sit with Jillian—there was nothing demanding about her."

How does Jillian affect Jane today?

I think of her, and I miss her when I see the dogwood blooming or see lavender—something that reminds me of her. When push comes to shove and I need to remember what really matters in life, not what is logical or rational—when one of those life questions comes up, Jillian's life helps me get my head on straight or helps me not get lost in the ways of the world. When you think about Jillian, there is a lot to ponder.

Jillian and her caregivers (clockwise from top): Kristina, Jane and Christine (standing) with Rachel on Jillian's lap, Mary Britton, and Jennifer at Niagara Falls.

NOTES

Chapter 1

1. Lewis, C. S. *A Grief Observed.* New York, New York: Bantam Books, 1976. 3.
2. Piper, John. "Today's Mercies for Today's Troubles." *The Elizabeth Elliot Newsletter*, March 13, 1994. Accessed April 4, 2015. http://www.desiringgod.org/resource-library/sermons/todays-mercies-for-todays-troubles.

Chapter 2

1. Lucado, Max. "Your Place at God's Table." Max Lucado. Accessed April 4, 2015. https://maxlucado.com/read/topical/your-place-at-gods-table/.

Chapter 3

1. Hurnard, Hannah. *Hinds' Feet on High Places*. Living Books ed. Wheaton, Ill.: Living Books, 1986. 145.

Chapter 4

1. Frankl, Viktor E. *Man's Search for Meaning*. 1st ed. Boston: Beacon Press, 2006. 65, 67.
2. Nouwen, Henri J. M. *The Wounded Healer: Ministry in Contemporary Society*. NY, NY: Image Books, 1990. 72.
3. Hazard, David. *Early Will I Seek You: A 40-day Journey in the Company of Augustine: Devotional Readings*. Minneapolis, Minn.: Bethany House, 1991. 38.
4. Hazard, David. *A Day in Your Presence: A 40-day Journey in the Company of Francis of Assisi: Devotional Readings.* Minneapolis, Minn.: Bethany House Publishers, 1992. 70.
5. Hazard, David. *You Set My Spirit Free: A 40-day Journey in the Company of John of the Cross: Devotional Readings.* Minneapolis, Minn.: Bethany House, 1994. 23-25.

6. De Vinck, Christopher. *The Power of the Powerless: A Brother's Legacy of Love*. NY: Crossroad Pub. 2002. 12.
7. De Vinck, *Power*. 85-87.
8. De Vinck, *Power*. 13.
9. Nouwen, Henri J. M. *The Road to Daybreak: A Spiritual Journey*. New York: Doubleday, 1988. 42.
10. De Vinck, *Power*. xviii.
11. Nouwen, *Daybreak*. 84.
12. Nouwen, *Daybreak*. 31.
13. Nouwen, *Daybreak*. 38.
14. *Christian Catalyst Collection: Henri Nouwen*. The Netherlands: Vision Video, 1996. DVD.
15. Nouwen, *Daybreak*. 97-98
16. *Christian Catalyst Collection: Henri Nouwen*. The Netherlands: Vision Video, 1996. DVD
17. Nouwen, Henri J. M. *In the Name of Jesus: Reflections on Christian Leadership*. New York: Crossroad, 1989. 28.
18. Buechner, Frederick. *Listening to Your Life: Daily Meditations with Frederick Buechner*. San Francisco: HarperSanFrancisco, 1992. 80.
19. Hazard, David. *Majestic Is Your Name: A 40-day Journey in the Company of Theresa of Avila: Devotional Readings*. Minneapolis, Minn.: Bethany House Publishers, 1993. 106-7.

Chapter 6

1. Martin, Jennifer. “The Lame Can Dance.” 2004.

Chapter 7

1. Rice, Chris. “Untitled Hymn (Come to Jesus).” Rocketown Records. 2003.

Books That Helped Me on My Journey

Books about people with special needs

Christopher de Vinck: *The Power of the Powerless*

Henri Nouwen: *The Road to Daybreak*

Henri Nouwen: *In the Name of Jesus*

Henri Nouwen: *Adam: God's Beloved*

Pamela Rosewell: *The Five Silent Years of Corrie Ten Boom*

Jean Vanier: *Community and Growth*

Books about suffering

Dietrich Bonhoeffer: *Letters and Papers from Prison*

Joy Dawson: *Some of the Ways of God in Healing: How to Get Answers and Directions When You're Suffering*

Viktor E. Frankl: *Man's Search for Meaning*

Nancy Guthrie: *Holding onto Hope: A Pathway Through Suffering to the Heart of God*

C.S. Lewis: *A Grief Observed*

Henri Nouwen, Donald P. Mcneill, and Douglas A. Morris: *Compassion: A Reflection on the Christian Life*

Henri Nouwen: *Can You Drink this Cup?*

Penelope Wilcock: *The Hawk and the Dove* (fiction)

Books about spiritual growth

Ken Gire: *Windows of the Soul*

Hannah Hurnard: *Hinds Feet on High Places*

Phillip W. Keller: *A Shepherd Looks at Psalm 23*

Keri Wyall Kent: *Breathe: Creating Space for God in a Hectic Life*

Mrs. E. Prentiss: *Stepping Heavenward: One Woman's Journey to Godliness*

Richard A. Swenson: *Margin: Restoring Emotional, Physical, Financial, and Time Reserves to Overloaded Lives*

Spiritual classics

Keith Beasley-Topliffe: *The Soul's Delight: Selected Writings of Evelyn Underhill* (Upper Room Spiritual Classics, Series 2)

David Hazard: *Rekindling the Inner Fire* series

Early Will I Seek You: A 40-Day Journey in the Company of Augustine

You Set My Spirit Free: A 40-Day Journey in the Company of John of the Cross

Your Angels Guard My Steps: A 40-Day Journey in the Company of Bernard of Clairvaux

A Day in Your Presence: A 40-Day Journey in the Company of Francis of Assisi

I Promise You a Crown: A 40-Day Journey in the Company of Julian of Norwich

Majestic Is Your Name: A 40-Day Journey in the Company of Theresa of Avila

Watchman Nee: *The Release of the Spirit*

John Skinner: *The Confession of Saint Patrick*

Corrie Ten Boom: *Tramp for the Lord*

Esther de Waal: *Seeking God: The Way of St. Benedict*

Daily meditations

Frederick Buechner: *Listening to Your Life*

Amy Carmichael: *Thou Givest, They Gather*

Amy Carmichael: *Edges of His Ways: Selections for Daily Reading*

Henri Nouwen: Any collection of writings